SALESMANSHIP Made Simple

The Made Simple series
has been created
especially for self-education
but can equally well
be used as
an aid to group study.
However complex the subject,
the reader is taken
step by step,
clearly and methodically,
through the course. Each volume
has been prepared by
experts,
taking account of
modern educational requirements,
to ensure the most
effective way of
acquiring knowledge.

In the same series

Accounting
Acting and Stagecraft
Additional Mathematics
Administration in Business
Advertising
Anthropology
Applied Economics
Applied Mathematics
Applied Mechanics
Art Appreciation
Art of Speaking
Art of Writing
Biology
Book-keeping
British Constitution
Business and Administrative
  Organisation
Business Economics
Business Statistics and Accounting
Calculus
Chemistry
Childcare
Commerce
Company Law
Computer Programming
Computers and Microprocessors
Cookery
Cost and Management Accounting
Data Processing
Dressmaking
Economic History
Economic and Social Geography
Economics
Effective Communication
Electricity
Electronic Computers
Electronics
English
English Literature
Export
Financial Management
French
Geology
German

Housing, Tenancy and Planning
  Law
Human Anatomy
Human Biology
Italian
Journalism
Latin
Law
Management
Marketing
Mathematics
Modern Biology
Modern Electronics
Modern European History
Modern Mathematics
Money and Banking
Music
New Mathematics
Office Practice
Organic Chemistry
Personnel Management
Philosophy
Photography
Physical Geography
Physics
Practical Typewriting
Psychiatry
Psychology
Public Relations
Rapid Reading
Retailing
Russian
Salesmanship
Secretarial Practice
Social Services
Sociology
Spanish
Statistics
Teeline Shorthand
Transport and Distribution
Twentieth-Century British
  History
Typing
Woodwork

SALESMANSHIP Made Simple

B. Howard Elvy

Made Simple Books
HEINEMANN : London

© B. Howard Elvy, 1971

Made and printed in Great Britain by
Richard Clay (The Chaucer Press), Ltd., Bungay, Suffolk
for the publishers William Heinemann Ltd.,
10 Upper Grosvenor Street, London W1X 9PA

First edition, April 1971
Second edition, June 1975
Third edition, March 1978
Reprinted, July 1979
Reprinted, April 1981
Reprinted, April 1982

SBN 434 98470 1

Foreword

How do I become a sales representative? What does industrial selling entail? What are the qualifications and attributes needed for success in selling? These are some of the questions which every young man must ask who hopes to embark upon a career of salesmanship.

This book answers not only these questions, it provides a comprehensive introduction to the whole field of salesmanship, with especial emphasis on the techniques of selling to industry. These techniques, however, apply in all fields of salesmanship and each student will adapt them to his own needs. The text begins by discussing the suitability of the candidate for the career in general; then it discusses, step by step, the processes of job application and interview, the interview itself, and the attitude towards the job. It then deals with such topics as preparation for selling to industrial users, obtaining initial orders, obtaining repeat business, compiling and writing sales reports, handling complaints and account problems. The special methods of selling in the export field and in the retail trade are also fully discussed.

Salesmanship Made Simple is written primarily for self-study, but is of equal value to students attending schools and colleges studying for the Ordinary and Higher National Certificates and Diplomas in Business Studies of the Department of Education and Science, and also to those studying for the Diploma in Marketing of the Institute of Marketing.

B. HOWARD ELVY

To Joan

Table of Contents

CHAPTER ONE

DECIDE YOUR OWN SUITABILITY

The job of a company representative selling to industry is one of the most attractive which modern business can offer to young men with the ambition and enthusiasm to work hard and succeed. Progressive firms realize the importance of recruiting men with good selling potentialities and are prepared to pay attractive salaries and to offer liberal expense allowances, good holidays, private use of a company-owned car and other 'fringe' benefits. The status of the company 'rep', both in business and in social life, is one to which increasing numbers of young men aspire.

The purpose of this book is to instruct the would-be salesman how to approach his prospective employer in such a manner that he will stand a very good chance of landing the job and, having got the job, how to ensure that in the shortest time possible he will become a successful industrial salesman.

In fulfilling this purpose, emphasis has been placed on the techniques involved in selling to industry. The principles, however, are applicable to all forms of salesmanship, including the selling of a service (such as insurance) and selling in the retail trade.

Successful salesmen are not born, they are made. They are made, usually, only after years of learning in the hard school of experience. This book cannot teach you *everything* about selling, for even the most experienced and successful salesmen will tell you that they never cease to learn something about their job with every call they make. What it will do, however, is to point out some of the pitfalls and offer a number of suggestions which may assist you in making more rapid progress than is possible 'learning the hard way'.

Selling is essentially a matter of knowing how to deal with people. There is no magic formula, no mystique, in successful salesmanship. It is based on the exercise of a considerable amount of common sense and some elementary psychology.

The term 'psychological selling' has acquired a spurious and, on occasion, a sinister association. Yet all selling is based on psychology, if by that we mean the comprehension of the mental processes and the emotional reactions of human beings. There is certainly nothing mystical about trying to understand other people. In our family, social and working lives, we all try to reach some understanding of the people with whom we are in contact. We try to anticipate their reactions to what we may say or do. The only difference between the professional salesman and the rest of humanity is that he applies his understanding of other people to his daily work.

Similarly, there is nothing mystical about the professional buyer. We are all buyers every day of our lives. Every customer in every shop, cinema, petrol-station or hairdressing salon is a buyer, either of goods or of services. Every adult citizen in every civilized society must exercise the buying function to exist. When we speak of a professional buyer, we are referring to one whose job it is to exercise the buying function on behalf of a firm or organization. He does not become different from his fellow men because he earns his living as a buyer. He remains an ordinary man, with all the strength and all the weakness, all the pride and all the prejudice, all the wisdom and all the folly which each of us, in varying measure, possesses.

Undoubtedly he acquires an expertise in the way in which he exercises the buying function, but the manner in which he performs his duties will depend on the kind of person he is. The successful salesman is one who can recognize the kind of person with whom he is dealing and who can, therefore, modify his approach to suit the particular personality and the particular circumstances of each individual buyer.

Whether he is selling a sophisticated chemical product or a tin of biscuits, the first hurdle the salesman must face is that of selling himself to his prospective customer. There is nothing new in this assertion, but I make no apology for restating it: it is fundamental to success in selling.

This is why, at the outset, I am going to ask you to assess your own suitability for a career in industrial selling. It may seem a strange request at the beginning of a book designed to instruct you how to succeed as a salesman. My reason for doing so is simple. Your task is to convince. First, you must convince your prospective employer that you are the right man for the job. Secondly, as a sales representative, you must convince your customer that you have something to say which is worth listening to, something to sell which is worth buying. Finally, you must convince your customer that, in dealing with you and the company which you represent, he is going to get a good product and good service over the months and years ahead.

Before you can hope to convince anyone else, you have first to convince yourself. You have to be sure, deep down within yourself, that you can do this job. Once you are so convinced, the rest is a matter of knowledge and experience. These you will acquire with effort and with time. But all the time and effort in the world will be fruitless if, within yourself, you are not convinced that you have the basic suitability for the career on which you wish to embark.

In reaching a decision on your suitability you must be completely honest with yourself. Read the whole book before you finally make up your mind. If at the end of it you decide that the life of a sales 'rep' is not for you, your time will not have been wasted. It will have saved you from much heartache and frustration. It will have saved you from wasting what may be precious months or years at a vital stage of your career. There are many opportunities in industry and commerce today, and not everybody is suited by nature to make a good salesman. Equally, however, the majority of good salesmen know, in their hearts, that they would probably make a poor showing in most other roles in the business world. A good salesman, in fact, is seldom much good at anything else. This is an indication of the rare qualities which the first-class industrial salesman must possess.

In your consideration of suitability, the following points should be considered.

Age

The company 'rep' selling to industry will, in fact, be selling to managers and directors. He must be able, personally, to meet his customers on something approaching equal terms. The very young man, therefore, is at an obvious disadvantage when dealing with men of senior position within their firms, who will probably be in their 40's or 50's. I would not consider seriously an applicant under 24–25 years of age as a sales representative unless he displayed a considerable degree of maturity for his age. This is in spite of the fact that the 'youngster' on occasion has the advantage over the older man, in that his obvious youth may make his middle-aged customers feel that they are helping a young man to get started.

Anyone over 30 who has not previously had selling experience might equally find it difficult to break into industrial selling with a progressive company. Such firms are looking for the man who above all wants to sell, and an applicant of 30 who has not sold before has either tried for a position elsewhere and been considered unsuitable or has never before had the urge to try his hand at selling.

The best age to go into industrial selling, therefore, is between 24 and 27. At this age the applicant has sufficient maturity, yet lack of previous experience cannot reasonably be held against him.

Health

Employers will look carefully at the health record of the potential representative. Among the reasons for this are:

(*a*) The high cost of keeping a salesman on the road, calculated in salary and expenses, including the provision of the company-owned car.

(*b*) It is essentially a one-man job, difficult to understudy during illness. When the salesman is away ill his territory is not being covered, existing business may be lost and opportunities for new business missed.

(*c*) The salesman is out in all weathers and for a considerable part of his time he may be staying away from home.

(*d*) A man of poor health is not a good ambassador to send out to see customers.

(*e*) Reliability in the salesman is essential. The man of poor health is likely to be unreliable through no fault of his own. He may have to break appointments because he is 'off sick' and his employer can never be confident that he is on top of his job.

Education

Because of his contact with men of managerial status within client companies, the salesman must be able to converse intelligently. He must be able to grasp the essentials of the product he has to sell and understand the processes employed by his customers. An uneducated man will always be at a disadvantage. He will be the victim of prejudice, of narrowness of outlook.

The lack of a good education is not an impossible obstacle if the aspirant has been prepared to do something about it. However, a potential employer would not be unreasonable in thinking that a man who had reached 25 or 30 years of age, and had done nothing about his lack of education, was unsuitable material for selling his products.

High education accomplishment is not essential. The man with the singleness of purpose to study and reach academic distinction seldom has sufficient fluidity of mind to make a good salesman. He tends to be too wrapped up in his special interests and may find it difficult to adjust to the varying intelligence levels of his clients. Put bluntly, the dedicated 'swot' is seldom the 'all-rounder' type of person who can mix well with the wide variety of people he will meet as a sales representative.

Temperament

Temperament is difficult to assess in others and even more difficult to assess in oneself. The temperament of a good salesman is a combination of contrasts. It has been summarized best as the possession of two essential qualities: 'ego-drive' and 'empathy'.

Ego-drive means the overriding need within oneself to succeed. Success is a dominant urge, transcending all other considerations. We have all met the man with tremendous 'drive' who will stop at nothing to achieve his ends. Such a person is tireless in his work, refuses to be put off by any obstacle and will ride roughshod over other people to achieve his goal. The highly successful business tycoons who have risen from humble origins to become the bosses of great national and international organizations all possess this wonderful—and terrible—quality known as ego-drive.

On its own, ego-drive does not make a good salesman. The reasons are obvious. Such a man will make enemies of many of the people with whom he comes into contact. They may admire him but few will like him. Eventually his over-persistence, his obvious self-interest and his lack of feeling for others will build up a solid wall of resistance. Before a salesman can sell anything, he must first sell himself. No man will sell himself to others if he is disliked as a person.

That is why the quality of ego-drive must be combined with empathy. Empathy simply means the ability to understand and appreciate the other fellow's point of view. Those who possess this quality will be sympathetic to the feelings of other people and quick to sense their needs. For all his ego-drive, the good salesman, possessing empathy, will not ride rough-shod over his colleagues or his customers. While refusing to be put off from achieving the success which is so important to him, he will find means of reaching his goal without antagonizing others. His very under-standing of their position will enable him to avoid the clashes of interest and of personality which so often create unnecessary obstacles for the man who has ego-drive and nothing else.

The good salesman is a self-contained individual. He must be not only self-reliant but capable of being at peace within himself. Selling as an industrial representative is a lonely job. Not 'lonely' in any unhappy, dismal sense of the word. It is a job which one does alone. One is on one's own, not a part of a visible team. One is unaccompanied. Although the salesman is required to mix with his customers and to establish a friendly relationship with them, he can never allow himself to make intimate friendships with them. Although he is required to converse with them, probably over a wide range of subjects and interests, he must never unburden himself to them. So many of his private opinions, so much of his private knowledge, cannot be confided to his client. Many a whole day and, on occasion, several days he will be away from his home, his family, his colleagues and his personal, intimate friends. All this time he has to be able to keep his inner thoughts and personal feelings to him-self. If he cannot do this, if he must share these thoughts and feelings with others, if he has the urgent need for the company of other people 'to take him out of himself', he will not make a sales representative.

I have asked you to consider your own suitability and already I may have aroused doubts in your mind. Already you may feel that there is rather more to this job of selling to industry than you had realized. If that much has been achieved, well and good. I am not out to depress you, still less to put you off. We are talking about a career and a career entails a working lifetime. It is best to get the facts straight right from the start. Everyone knows the sunny side of a representative's life:

freedom from supervision, no clocking on and clocking off, being one's own master and riding around the countryside in a firm's car. All this is perfectly true, but there is the other side of the coin.

Please do not be depressed—at least, not yet. Although the requirements of age, health, education and temperament may seem somewhat daunting, remember that we all of us possess greater capacity than we ever know until it is put to the test. Many a man who has had an unlooked-for responsibility thrust upon him has found, to his surprise and delight, that he has been able to rise to the occasion far better than he ever thought he could. One grows into the kind of person which the job demands, providing one is prepared to understand what those demands are.

CHAPTER TWO

APPLYING FOR A POSITION

In this chapter we shall consider the various methods by which you may obtain a position as a sales representative. Before we do so, however, it will be as well to understand the purpose of the job which you hope to take.

Why Industrial Firms Need Sales Representatives

Very few of the products sold to the general public are the creation of a single manufacturer. A motor-car, a television set or a suite of furniture consists of a variety of components. So, for that matter, does a pocket torch, a fountain-pen or a box of chocolates. The range of materials required and the processing techniques employed are too diverse to be undertaken by any one manufacturer. The firm which produces the final product is therefore dependent upon a number of suppliers of materials and of components in order to carry out its own manufacturing processes. Few such suppliers have a monopoly of their markets. In the vast majority of cases they must compete with others similarly engaged in order to sell their products.

In highly industrialized societies, such as those of North America, Great Britain and Western Europe, the degree of competition between one manufacturer and another is often such that only the most economic methods of production will ensure survival. To achieve this required economy of production, high-volume output is essential. To maintain high-volume output, one obviously needs high-volume sales.

Furthermore, every manufacturing business has a 'break-even figure'.

This is the figure, in terms of output, which must be achieved before the overhead costs of running the business can be covered. To obtain a sufficient return on the capital which has been invested in its manufacturing plant and to cover its overheads, a firm must sell a certain minimum quantity of its products before it even begins to make a profit.

This constant demand for sales can only be met if the selling side of the organization is able to continue to obtain repeat orders from its existing customers and can gain new customers to replace those who, for a variety of reasons, cease to use its products.

It is to provide this steady intake of orders that the sales representative is employed. His task is to maintain sales by means of personal contact with his company's existing customers and to extend those sales by the establishment of business with new customers.

Everything else one may do as a sales representative is subordinate to this prime function of keeping one's manufacturing plant fed with a regular supply of orders. If the flow of orders stops, the machines stop; profits disappear, the labour force becomes redundant and there is no money to pay the wages and salaries of the sales staff. This is the area representative's degree of responsibility and it can, at times, be a heavy one.

It will be seen that the representative is a vital cog in the wheel of modern industry. He is the link between supplier and user at every stage from the basic raw material to the final product. The importance of industrial salesmen is recognized by the status which industry accords them. If you aspire to join their ranks, there are several avenues of approach and, in considering these, you should first select your particular industry and then your particular company.

Select the Industry

It has been suggested that the minimum age for entry into industrial selling is about 24. It may be assumed that the aspirant has been gainfully employed for some years previously and it is likely that this employment has been in an industrial organization of some kind. When he starts to think about how he can sell himself to an employer, therefore, one of the things in the applicant's favour will be some knowledge of the industry in which he is already engaged.

This may not necessarily apply. The industry in which he is currently working may not particularly interest him. It is important that he should make up his mind at the outset as to which type of industrial activity most appeals to him. As a salesman he will find his work intrinsically more rewarding if he is genuinely interested in the products and processes with which he will be involved for several years to come.

In selecting your industry you should, of course, temper your personal interest with a consideration of the scope which any particular industry may have to offer. Obviously the scope for advancement of the individual will be greater in some spheres than in others. To take a few examples, it would seem probable that the building, petro-chemical and packaging industries will continue to expand; the electrical engineering, domestic appliance and leathergoods industries may remain static or even decline over a period of years.

Select the Company

Having selected the industry which appeals to you and in which you believe there is scope for expansion, you should next consider the selection of a company. It is of course most important that before you join a firm you should know something about it. It is not simply a question of getting a job: the job must be worth while once you have got it. The remuneration and the fringe benefits are not the only factors to be considered for these can probably be paralleled by a number of companies within a particular industry. What really matters is the financial standing of the firm, its stability and its potential for expansion. Upon these factors will rest your future security, your chances of promotion and the realization of any ambitions you have for management status in the years to come.

Very often one comes across a smallish company which offers to employ inexperienced men and to train them to sell its goods at an attractive salary. Occasionally, such a firm thrives and prospers and those who join its ranks in the early days, taking much that is offered to them on trust, grow with the company and enjoy their just rewards in after years when they hold well paid and influential positions.

There are other companies, however, which could be unstable financially. They may not have the resources to expand the scope of their activities in keeping with market demands. These are the firms that get left behind in the commercial race. To work as a salesman for such a firm may get you a living—but little else. It will rob you of the opportunity and the challenge of competing on equal terms with your competitors. It can be an unrewarding and, at times, an embittering experience. Too many young men of promise blight their careers by entering industrial selling through the wrong door. There is a considerable demand by good firms for good salesmen. The best advice one can give to an aspirant is to take a long look at a company before he joins it.

Four Methods of Approach

(a) Personal Recommendation

If you have a personal contact within a suitable firm, or can obtain an introduction, you may be able to gain an entry without having to wait until a vacancy occurs. Industrial companies are always on the lookout for likely men whom they can train as salesmen and for future managerial positions. They may not have an immediate vacancy, but if a suitable person presents himself they may well decided to take him on. Sooner or later their expansion may necessitate more staff; meanwhile they might set him to work under a senior representative as an assistant.

There are certain disadvantages in joining a company as the result of influence. One may be regarded by one's colleagues with a degree of suspicion. If one acquires a position which, in other circumstances, may have been open to members of the existing staff, some resentment could result. Furthermore, the man who has 'got there only because he knew somebody' is bound to lack the confidence which springs from knowing that one has got the job purely on one's own merits. Both these considerations are highly relevant. A salesman needs the willing support of his colleagues, especially the 'inside men' of the sales office. Above all, the novice salesman requires all the self-confidence he can muster and anything which tends to sap that confidence will be a big disadvantage.

There is another avenue of approach which we may consider at this stage and which is not dependent upon one's personal connections. There is nothing to prevent you from writing to one or more companies operating in the industry of your choice, telling them that you are seeking the position of a sales representative, giving a brief description of your education and business career to date, and asking for an interview. This approach has been known to produce good results. Some of the firms to whom you write may have a full complement of staff and yet may be willing to bear you in mind should the situation alter. There may be at least one or two who would be willing to grant you an interview and, if this showed you to be the right material, you could be taken on as a trainee.

(b) Staff Employment Agencies

The staff employment agencies are not a very fruitful field for those seeking positions as sales representatives. Generally speaking such agencies fall into two categories: those which deal with office staff, typists, clerks and book-keepers; and those which specialize in the recruitment of experienced personnel to fill professional and managerial positions. The selection of inexperienced men who may be suitable for training as salesmen is not a task which can be delegated to a third party.

(c) Internal Promotion

Many firms prefer to draw their trainee salesmen from the ranks of their existing staff wherever this is possible. There are obvious advantages to the employer who has known a man over a period of months or years and can form an assessment in depth of his character and capabilities. It is also good for the general morale of the inside staff to know that they will be considered for promotion to outside selling should the opportunity arise.

If you are already employed in some junior technical or clerical capacity within an industrial organization and desire to become a salesman you should make your ambitions known to your superiors. If, in their opinion, you 'have what it takes', sooner or later an opportunity should occur for them to consider you.

On the other hand, there are situations where a good inside man finds his opportunities for transfer to the sales staff obstructed by the head of his department who does not want to lose him. This is both unfair and short-sighted. If the man really has 'what it takes' to make a salesman, he will not be put off indefinitely. He will move to another firm where his potentialities are given greater scope for expression.

(d) Press Advertisements

It is as the result of advertisements in the newspapers that the majority of salesmen are recruited. Many job advertisements in the 'classified' columns of newspapers contain little indication of the nature of the work involved, the industry to be served or the area to be covered. In some cases the firm disguises its identity behind a Box Number. Should you decided to apply for a position which has been advertised in this manner, it would be as well to exercise some caution. The term 'sales representative' has no exact definition and there are, regrettably, some organizations whose terms of employment of so-called representatives may need careful examination.

However, major companies take great care over specifying their requirements when advertising for salesmen and almost without exception include their name and address in the announcement. Their candour is an assurance that the vacancies offered are genuine and that all personal details disclosed in response to such advertisements will be treated in strict confidence.

Writing the Letter of Application

On the assumption that you are likely to seek employment as a sales representative by means of a Press advertisement, let us examine a typical announcement.

THE SUPER-COLOSSAL PLASTICS COMPANY

have vacancies for

SALES REPRESENTATIVES

Due to our expansion programme we are seeking young people aged 24–30 years, preferably with some experience in plastics, to train as representatives. Successful applicants will be appointed to territories in the Midlands and the Southern Counties.
Remuneration will be subject to negotiation.
A Company-owned car will be provided.
Applications, in writing only, to:

The Sales Manager,
Super-Colossal Plastics Company,
Barchester.

This kind of advertisement, which might appear in the 'quality' newspapers, does not say much—but what it does say should be studied carefully before you write your letter. There are two vital questions to be asked: (a) what kind of person is the advertiser looking for and (b) why should *you* be considered for the job?

(a) What Kind of Applicant Is Required?

The advertisement offers us only two clues to the kind of man the firm is seeking. He has to be within the age limit of 24–30 years. This, surely, is only an indication. A mature 23 year old or a keen and energetic 31-year-old is hardly likely to be debarred on age alone. Obviously, however, the firm is not likely to consider a man of 19 or one close to 40.

The second point is that the applicant should have some knowledge of plastics. The word 'preferably' indicates that this is not essential. No previous selling experience has been demanded. It may be assumed, therefore, that since training will be given no sales or product knowledge is essential. If your age lies between the early twenties and the early thirties, this is a job for which you could apply.

(b) Why Should You Be Considered?

Because the stated requirements of the advertiser are so broad, he is likely to receive a large number of replies from hopeful applicants. What chance, you may ask, will you have, with little or no knowledge of plastics and no sales experience to recommend you?

I would prefer you to ask yourself: what do I possess, in the way of knowledge, experience, previous training or special capabilities which might lead to my being considered for this job? We said at the outset that, above all, the salesman must be able to sell himself. You should now put your inherent selling ability to the test.

The piece of paper on which you write your letter of application will be the only ambassador representing you to your potential employer. On this piece of paper you must present yourself in such away as to impress the man who receives it that you are just the person he is looking for.

Very few people know how to write the kind of letter of application which will be certain of gaining them an interview. Men with good qualifications and experience fail to land a job because they do not write a good letter. They may have good personalities but do not put this across in their writing.

A potential employer usually makes a 'short list' of 'possibles', selected from the letters of application which he receives in response to his advertisement. These are the applicants to whom he will grant an interview. Your letter must get you on to that 'short list'.

Put yourself in the position of the man who will read your letter. He is likely to be the sales manager of the organization and, therefore, a busy person with many calls upon his time. The selection and appointment of salesmen is an additional task imposed on him when the need arises to replace or increase his sales team. He probably has a fair idea of the type of person he is looking for. The sooner he can find the right man and engage him, the sooner he can get on with his other important work.

Staff selection is a time-consuming chore. The sales manager will avoid having to interview a large number of men. Each interview will probably last about 30 minutes. This means that at most only two appointments can be arranged per hour and, if he short-lists 12 applicants, he must devote a solid six hours to interviewing. If his secretary books the first appointment at 10 a.m., he will be interviewing, with a short break for lunch, until late afternoon. In other words he will have to spend a whole working day just interviewing 12 applicants. If none of these proves suitable, he will have to see another batch of 12 and yet another day will be taken up. In the week of his interviews, therefore, the sales manager will have devoted at least one day (20 per cent of his working time) merely to seeing possible applicants. Little wonder that he will keep his short list as short as possible. That is why your letter *must* be effective.

Remember, that although you may be reasonably satisfied with your career to date, your ideas of success may not match those of the man to whom you are writing. He has risen to a position of responsibility. He will undoubtedly be earning considerably more than you. Do not expect him to be impressed by your achievements just because you are impressed by them yourself.

On the other hand, do not be humble in your letter. Write respectfully, but do not over-emphasize your respect. Avoid the use of clichés about 'not being afraid of hard work' or 'giving of your best'. If you get the job it goes without saying that your employer will expect you to work hard and give of your best. Telling him so in advance will not impress him. He is looking for personality and intelligence and the personable and intelligent individual does not 'soft-soap' a potential employer in this obvious way.

For the purposes of illustration, let us assume for the applicant an identity, a background and some comparatively slight commercial experience. If we leaven the whole with a few outside interests which may not be improbable, the facts might look like this:

Name of Applicant:	John William Smith
Date of Birth:	1st April 19..
Place of Birth:	London, England
Marital Status:	Single

Education:	Oxbridge Secondary Modern School, Oxbridge
	'O' level passes in English literature, Geography and History.
	Midtown Technical College (Evening Classes), Midtown
	'O' level passes in Mathematics and English Language.
Employment:	Nuts and Bolts Ltd., High Street, Oxbridge: as Sales Correspondence Clerk.
	Brace and Bit Ltd., Canal Street, Midtown: as assistant to the Commercial Manager.
Personal Interests:	Oxbridge Amateur Dramatic Society; chess; walking; reading; the theatre.

Before we write John William Smith's letter of application I should like you to read a few letters which are not untypical of the kind of response one might receive from the advertisement reproduced on page 11.

EXAMPLE 1

'I would refer you to your advertisement in this week's *Daily Sentinel* which calls for Sales Representatives.

'I am 24 years of age and would be most grateful if you would consider me for this position.

'I was educated at Barchester Grammar School and am at present employed by a company in the metal industry. I have had experience of plastics materials though only from the office sales side.

'I trust that this application is of interest to you and I await your reply.

Yours faithfully,

I wonder what you make of that letter. The applicant has said only three things about himself:

(*a*) his age;

(*b*) that he had a grammar-school education;

(*c*) that he is at present employed in the sales office of a metal firm and has some knowledge of plastic materials.

No personality comes over, and the employer has virtually nothing to go on.

What did the applicant do at school?
What subjects did he study? Did he gain any distinction in any of them?
Did he (does he) play any games?
What did he do when he left school?
How long has he been with his present firm? In what capacity?
What are his ambitions?
In a nutshell, why does he think he should be considered?

EXAMPLE 2

'I refer to your advertisement in the *Daily Sentinel*.

'I would like to take this opportunity of applying for the post of representative in your company. I have had over four years' experience with my present employers, whose business is the wholesaling of foam rubber to manufacturing and retail outlets in Southern England.

'I am 30 years of age, married, with a family. As there is no more advancement in my present company, I hope your company will offer better prospects than I am able to procure at present.

Yours faithfully,

This application is only slightly better than the first example. The writer tells us that:
(*a*) he is 30 years old;
(*b*) he is a family man;
(*c*) he has had four years with his present firm, which is involved in selling foam rubber;
(*d*) he gives a reason for wanting to make a change (there are no more prospects for him).

Would you interview this man?

EXAMPLE 3

'With reference to your advertisement in the *Daily Sentinel* for a Sales Representative, I would like to apply for the position.

'I am 25 years old and I have been driving for eight years and hold a clean driving licence.

'I left school at 16 after obtaining two passes at G.C.E. 'O' level.

'My first position was with a company manufacturing motor accessories, as a Sales Clerk for three years. I then moved on to become assistant to the Sales Manager in a company making plastic containers for four years.

'I have been in my present position, where I am in control of the Sales Office of a firm of hardware merchants, for 15 months.

'I await your earliest convenience.

Yours faithfully,

This man tells us a little more than the other two. We know that:

(*a*) he is 25 years old;

(*b*) he has been driving for eight years and holds a licence without endorsement;

(*c*) he left school at 16 with two 'O' level passes;

(*d*) he has had experience in the sales departments of three different firms;

(*e*) he stayed in one job for three years and another for four years.

The fact which we have to remember is that each of the above letters was written by a person who wanted to be considered as a salesman. Not one of them has grasped the idea that he must first sell himself to his potential employer.

Now let us set out the letter of application of John William Smith, whose personal details we outlined previously.

'I refer to your advertisement in the *Daily Sentinel* and wish to be considered for the position of a Sales Representative.

'My age is twenty-four. I am single and had a good general education at the Oxbridge Secondary Modern School where I obtained 'O' level passes in English Literature, Geography and History. After leaving school at the age of sixteen, I continued my studies at the Midtown Technical College by attending Evening Classes and ultimately obtained 'O' level passes in Mathematics and English Language.

'For the past six years I have been engaged in industrial selling, as a Sales Correspondence Clerk with Nuts and Bolts, Ltd. of Oxbridge and, latterly, as the assistant to the Commercial Manager of Brace and Bit Ltd. of Midtown. My duties have brought me into contact with customers by letter and telephone. Unfortunately, there is little scope for me to handle direct sales negotiations in person since these are normally dealt with by the directors of this comparatively small firm.

'I am, therefore, seeking to broaden my knowledge and experience by taking the position of a Sales Representative with a larger organization.

'My knowledge of the plastics industry, I must admit, is extremely slender. However, I knew nothing of the metal industry when I entered it five years ago and within that time I feel I have acquired a considerable understanding of its processes and marketing methods. With the training which you offer I am sure that I shall obtain an equal appreciation of the requirements of the plastics industry.

'My career details are itemized for your convenience on the attached sheet.

'Outside my business activities, I am a member of the local amateur dramatics society, am a moderate chess player and enjoy walking, reading and the theatre.

'I hope you will accord me the opportunity of an interview.

Yours faithfully,

The qualifications and experience which John William Smith has been able to offer differ very little from those of the authors of the previous letters. I think you will agree, however, that he has put himself over rather better than they. He has written an interesting letter, one which has a certain style about it. It is detectable, I believe, that he might well have quite a good opinion of himself, but this is one of the attributes one must look for in a salesman. Above all, by setting out as much about himself as he has, he has provided the employer with some glimpse of the kind of man he might be.

This letter should get John William Smith his interview.

CHAPTER THREE

SELL YOURSELF AT THE INTERVIEW

How to Prepare for the Interview

If you possess intelligence and imagination, it is inevitable that you will approach your interview with your prospective employer with a degree of apprehension. Much will depend upon its outcome. If the job for which you have applied is the one you particularly want you may well be suffering acute anxiety as the fatal hour approaches. You will wonder what questions you may be asked and whether you will be able to find the right answers. You may have heard that some interviewers have a stock of 'trick' questions and you will wonder what these are and whether you will recognize them when they come. Above all, you may be fearful that you will not match up to the interviewer's requirements and that your golden opportunity will be lost.

Although your hypertension is unlikely to be abated, some of the unnecessary worry which attaches to an employment interview can be removed if you will give some quiet thought, in advance, to what the interviewer is seeking.

Until you have met the man who will interview you, it is obvious that you cannot be sure of the manner he will adopt or what your own reactions are likely to be. You can, however, put yourself, in imagination, into the position of the interviewer and give some thought to the kind of questions he is likely to ask. This pre-interview mental preparation is something which you will have to learn to do before all important interviews in your working life as a sales representative. There are few interviews which will take place in your career which are likely to be of greater importance to you than the one which will secure for you your first job as a salesman.

The Company and its Products

One of the first things to do is to find out all you can about the firm and its products. Is it a private or a public company? Is it old-established or of recent origin? Is it part of a large group? If so, what are the other companies in the group? What does the company make? Where are its factories? Does it sell its products under brand names? If so, what are they? Who are its likely competitors?

'What do you know about our company and our products?' is almost a stock question of interviewers. What the interviewer is seeking is not the accuracy of your knowledge. All the necessary information on these subjects will be provided in the event of your getting the job. The point of the question is to discover whether you have made the effort to find out.

When a firm is reasonably well known in its industry and an applicant cannot say that he knows much about what it makes, its size, or where it is likely to sell its products, this man has obviously not given such matters a great deal of thought. The applicant who comes up with ideas of what he thinks the firm makes and where he thinks their markets lie may, very often, have the wrong facts. But the interviewer feels that at least he has anticipated the question, at least he has shown some initiative.

What the Interviewer is Seeking

Bear in mind that the interviewer will be trying to find out as much about you as he can in a very limited period of time. On the assumption you have no previous experience of industrial selling, he will not be looking for qualifications in the sense of prior knowledge of the job. He will be looking for some potential in you which, with training and experience, will enable you to acquire the necessary aptitude and attitude that the job requires. He will try to build a picture of you and of your life so far. His basic questions will, therefore, relate to your education, where you grew up, what sort of work you have done and what your interests are. He will only establish this picture from what you say and the way in which you say it.

There is often uncertainty in the minds of young job applicants as to how far they should 'push' themselves during an interview. They are, naturally, anxious to show the best side of themselves and yet are often inhibited by a fear of saying the wrong thing or saying too much. They are afraid of 'catch' questions. Sometimes, they react as though they suspect that every question, however innocently asked, is designed to trap them into denouncing themselves.

I recall an occasion when, in order to put a young applicant at his ease, I asked him how he was. He looked disconcertedly at me and hesitated to make a reply. I had to explain to him that 'not every question is loaded'.

The only way to deal with this problem is to consider what the interviewer is really seeking. In general, your prospective employer is looking for three basic qualities: (a) intelligence, (b) personality and (c) what, for want of a better word, I will call honesty. He can only form an opinion of you on these three counts by getting you to express yourself.

The Art of Self-projection

From the moment you step into the interview room, you have to project yourself. By this, I do not mean that you should grip the interviewer's hand like a vice and become highly voluble. The last thing which an employer is looking for is a bad stage caricature of a commercial traveller. He is seeking a man who will be his ambassador to his customers, who will create goodwill and sell his products. You have to give him the impression that you are the kind of person who will measure up to these requirements.

By projection of your personality, I do not mean acting a part. If the interviewer has any experience of people, he will soon detect that it is an act. At all times and in all circumstances, you must remain yourself. Everyone, at some time or another, wishes that he could alter his personality. But, for good or ill, this cannot be done without artifice and the result is a transparent 'phoneyness' which will deceive neither a shrewd employer nor a shrewd customer.

All that you have to project is yourself, with all those blemishes of which you are so conscious and, also, all those qualities of which you may be unaware. If the interviewer does not like the real you, then you must consider it just too bad. We all have our prejudices about other people and, if your face does not fit with the interviewer, you must, on this occasion, consider yourself doomed. There will be other days and other interviews.

It is the *one and only you* that has to be projected. It is important that you should understand this because the interview for the job is only the beginning. If you are going to be a salesman, you will have to go on projecting yourself, day after day, year after year, every time you meet a new customer. In time it will become automatic.

Your First Sale is Yourself

I said earlier that the salesman has to sell himself. Think of yourself as a saleable commodity. Decide how you would go about selling a commodity to a man who was sufficiently interested that he had asked to see it, but who was reserving his judgment about buying it until he had sized it up and decided whether or not it would meet his requirements and was worth the price he would have to pay for it.

Your prospective employer wants to buy himself a salesman. He wants a young man, of good appearance, who can speak up for himself. He wants someone who is of a cheerful rather than a dismal disposition. He is looking for a degree of self-confidence but he abhors any sign of brashness. He does not like conceit but, at the same time, he expects a man to have a reasonably good opinion of himself. He will appreciate a sign of natural good manners, provided that they are natural and not put on merely to impress him.

The interviewer will ask you something of your background. Where were you born? What schools did you attend? What educational attainments have you? What was your first job? Tell him and tell him truthfully. State the facts, adding any explanations which you consider to be relevant. Remember one thing: it is your life which you are discussing. Do not apologize for it. Do not imply that you are apologizing for it. This is what I mean by showing that you have a reasonably good opinion of yourself. If you did not do so well at school, if you failed your examinations, you do not have to spell the fact out to him. The fact that you were no great scholar will not prevent you from being a good salesman. Do not despair about it, and do not let the interviewer feel that you despair about it. Let him realize that past failures have not undermined your belief in your future success.

Do not be in too much of a hurry to agree with everything that the interviewer says. Sometimes an employer will deliberately make some provocative remark merely to draw the applicant out and to see what his reaction will be. This is where the quality of honesty comes in. You are entitled to a contrary opinion. I am not suggesting that you should argue with the interviewer over a trivial point. Nor should you contradict him on a matter of fact unless it is vital and concerns the proposed appointment. But if he has chosen to turn the conversation to a discussion of some general issue, it is likely that he is genuinely seeking your views. This is a matter for your judgment. If you have a different viewpoint, by all means express it. Let him know that you have opinions, that you are not just a 'yes-man'. Remember, however, that he will be judging you not only in the context of this conversation but also in the light of possible future conversations which you may have with his customers. No reasonably minded individual resents the expression of an opposing viewpoint, if he has invited it, provided that it is expressed in polite terms and devoid of rancour and prejudice.

The interviewer is likely to ask you what your aims are in life. Try to be specific. Tell him that you want a job which will provide you with a good income and a degree of security. A job which carries with it the opportunity, in time, for promotion to some form of managerial responsibility. Above all, you want a job that will be demanding and, therefore, always interesting.

You may feel that this sounds a little trite. There is certainly nothing original in the expression of such ambitions. Your justification for expressing them is that in all probability they will be true. If you feel that the interviewer has received them with a degree of cynicism you may relax with the thought that you have at least shown him that you knew the right answer.

Remuneration and Expenses

Starting salaries and 'fringe benefits' are fairly consistent throughout British industry today. Generally, a trainee salesman's salary will depend on his past earnings, his age, and whether he is married or single.

Where a commission system is in operation, the basic salary will be lower. Commission arrangements can vary widely between one industry and another. They are usually calculated on the turnover achieved in the territory, for which the salesman is responsible, in excess of a basic figure. This basic figure may, for an established territory, equal the turn-over figure of previous years, thus ensuring that the salesman will draw commission only on the new business which he achieves. Commission may be paid on a monthly, a quarterly or an annual basis.

As a novice sales representative, entering an industry which may be unfamiliar to you, you may find it difficult to assess your likely gross earnings if part of your remuneration is to be based on commission. A reputable firm pays commission as an incentive. It will aim to so arrange the salesman's remuneration that he will receive a fair pay for the work which he is doing. The employer will take into account the likely increase in business in the proposed territory and, having set a basic salary and a rate of commission, will want the salesman to earn a good overall remuneration. A ceiling is usually placed on the amount of commission which the sales representative can earn in any one year.

It is most inadvisable for an inexperienced person to accept a job as a salesman on commission only. In your first few months you will be learning the job, and business may not come easily: you have to become known and accepted by your customers. Even when you are established, there will be seasonal variations in the level of business and the man who is solely dependent on commission earnings to feed and house his family can have a very worrying time. A firm which does not have sufficient confidence in you to pay you a regular basic salary should be viewed with suspicion and you can almost certainly obtain a better job elsewhere.

It is usual for a company-owned car to be provided. The company normally undertakes to tax and insure it, pays for all servicing and repair bills and for all petrol consumed in travelling on the firm's business. The salesman is usually allowed free use of the vehicle at week-ends and for holiday travel in the United Kingdom; he is, of course, expected to pay for all petrol and oil used for such private motoring. The salesman is expected to garage the car at his own expense and to keep it in good condition.

All expenses incurred on the company's business, including hotel bills, rail travel and customer entertaining, are usually paid by the company. Some firms provide their salesmen with an initial 'float'. Generally, expenses are reimbursed at the end of each month.

CHAPTER FOUR

BEFORE YOU START—SOME ESSENTIAL PREPARATIONS

Industrial companies nowadays normally arrange for newly engaged sales representatives to receive some basic training in the product to be sold. The degree of training provided varies considerably. Some very large, internationally known firms maintain training centres staffed with qualified instructors. They take the trainee salesman through a course which covers every aspect of manufacture from the initial design stage through to packing and dispatch. In addition to product information, instruction is usually given in the methods by which the product should be sold. This includes an understanding of the sales policy of the company and the sales techniques which have been perhaps built up over many years. The salesman is often taught a selling formula and is expected to apply it when he goes out on the road.

Unfortunately, few firms are able to provide such comprehensive training. In the majority of companies the initial training consists of a few days spent at the production plant and a few more in the sales office; this is followed by a week or two 'outside' with one of the company's senior representatives, who will try to show the newcomer the accepted methods of approach. In a small or medium-sized firm the facilities simply do not exist to provide fully adequate training for new salesmen. Such companies do not recruit a sufficient number of trainees to warrant the expense involved. Nor do their experienced sales personnel have the time to devote to the task of instructing new recruits. Therefore the novice usually finds himself 'thrown in at the deep end' and is expected to learn to swim almost immediately after he has taken the plunge.

There are certain essential preparations which you will be well advised to make before starting on your first round of calls. What these preparations are we shall discuss in the remainder of this chapter.

Consider Your Product

It is obvious, when one thinks about it, that few products are entirely superlative. While it is right that you should have faith in the product which you are about to sell, it should not be blind faith. No product is likely to be entirely superlative, but it is equally true that no product already established on the market is likely to be wholly inadequate. All products marketed by industrial companies lie somewhere between these extremes. It is on the basis of this assumption that you should decide the competitive merit of the product which you are required to sell.

(a) Attributes: What Advantages Can You Offer to Attract Sales?

What are the selling points of your product? In other words, how is it better than the products offered by your competitors? This is one of the questions which, before you go out into your territory, you should ask your sales management. One might assume that it would be covered in even the most meagre form of basic training, yet it is a subject that is seldom considered in sufficient depth by the majority of new salesmen. Too often it is imagined that, because the management of one's company is enthusiastic about the product and because it is already being sold in the market, one has only to introduce it to a sufficient number of new customers to obtain orders. This is the blind-faith snare mentioned above. Many novices believe, or are led to believe by their own management, that the market is waiting for their product and that it will sell itself if offered widely enough. A rude awakening awaits the tyro who accepts this fable.

Your product may be equally as good as that of your competitors, but this is only another way of saying it is no better. It may, however, be better in some ways although not in others. This is something you should establish before you go out to sell.

(b) Limitations: What Are Its Weaknesses?

Every product has some weakness, some disadvantage in comparison with those offered by competitors. If it is the finest of its kind technically, the cost of its production will, in all probability, make it slightly more expensive than its nearest rival. This will be its weakness in a highly competitive market. On the other hand it may be the cheapest on the market; but it will not have all the hallmarks of some of its competitors. It should be understood that a product may possess certain shortcomings without being unacceptable. The fact that a product continues to exist in the market for which it has been devised indicates that in spite of its limitations it is meeting at least some of the market's requirements. One must know where to draw the line, If, in ignorance of the limitations of his product, the salesman offers it for an application for which it is unsuitable, he risks bringing into disrepute not only his product but also his company and himself. Knowledge of the limitations of your product is essential before you go out to sell.

(c) Competitive Merit: On Balance, Why Should Customers Buy Your Product?

This is a matter of making an assessment based on a knowledge of attributes and limitations of the product. The customer should buy your product because of its attributes and because its limitations do not preclude its use for his particular purpose.

Successful industrial selling is largely a question of marrying a specific product to a specific application and the customer's particular needs. The customer may be buying from one of your competitors a product which, although similar to yours, has certain attributes not possessed by your component or material. Let us take as an example a certain type of lacquer paint. The competitor's paint, which the customer has been purchasing for some time, may be of a very consistent quality. It may dry to a very high gloss, be resistant to chipping and competitively priced.

At first sight, this particular piece of business would seem difficult to attack, especially if your competitor backs up his quality with a good delivery service. However, on the assumption that no product is entirely superlative, one should seek the possible weakness *so far as this application is concerned.* The answer could be that the drying time of the competitor's paint is slightly longer than that of the paint which your company is offering. For this particular customer's purposes, drying time may not matter much; on the other hand, it may cause him something of a problem. He may be spraying large cabinets on an assembly line. The cabinets may be dried in an oven. The length of time taken to dry the paint will affect the speed of the assembly line. If he could speed up his drying he might be able to speed up his entire assembly process and in doing so make some reduction in his manufacturing costs.

We have suggested that your company's paint has this attribute of shorter drying time. Possibly, however, the gloss of your paint is not quite as good as that of your competitor. If the customer had to assess the merit of the two qualities of paint purely on the basis of gloss he would probably reject yours. But with the advantages to be gained by using your paint, because of its faster drying, he may feel he can concede something on the question of gloss. He will accept a slightly inferior gloss to obtain cost savings on his final product brought about by the attribute which your paint has over that of your competitor, namely faster drying.

As a further example to illustrate the same point, let us assume you are a salesman for industrial adhesives. The customer's process is such that two components have to be stuck together. Your adhesive is sold at a lower price than that of your competitor. It has the same good adhesive permanence as the competitive product. It also has a particular property not enjoyed by the competitor: that of fast drying. On the basis of our previous example this particular attribute should enable you to win this business away from the other supplier. Undoubtedly, as a good salesman should, you will emphasize this advantage in your adhesive. But you find, when the customer tests it, that there is a snag. He has 20 women operatives working in his assembly shop. Ten of them are engaged in cutting into varying required lengths pieces of plastic strip used as trimming on certain cabinets. The work is so organized that they also apply the adhesive to the strip, which then passes to the next section where it is fixed round the cabinets. It would be inconvenient to his existing set-up and would create several problems if the customer had to alter this procedure. The snag he has found is that your fast-drying adhesive dries too fast: before the assembly stage is reached the adhesive on the decorative trim has dried hard and is completely useless.

These two examples illustrate the problems which arise in a consideration of the competitive merit of a product. Much wasted time and effort can be avoided by an understanding of the attributes and also the limitations of the product to be sold. Many opportunities can be created by knowing its competitive merits.

Consider Your Company

The next thing you should consider before you set out to sell is the situation of your company in relation to its competitors. As with the product, it is apparent that no company is entirely superlative. Every company has its strengths and its weaknesses and the balance which is struck between these two factors will establish its competitive merit in the market.

(a) Attributes

The old-established commercial firm has obvious attractions in the eyes of its customers and potential customers. Its longevity will have created an aura of stability, reliability and integrity. These are powerful attributes, bulwarks against the attack of less established competitors, firms new in the field and as yet unknown and untried. Users of industrial products rightly place emphasis on the stability and reliability of their suppliers. Business which is held, and has been held for many years, by a company whose name is a 'household word' in a particular industry may often appear, to its competitors, to be unassailable. If you happen to be employed as a salesman with such a firm you will begin with many advantages. The man who represents a well known and highly regarded company will always find it just that much easier to get a hearing. The resistance of buyers to the reception of new products is just that much less when the firm which is offering them is one of established reputation.

You may, however, be representing a company which, because it is new, is thrusting and progressive. It may well offer a better service to customers than the old-established firm which has become complacent

and inefficient. The policies of the new company may be more enlightened, more applicable to today's needs of the market, than those of
its longer-established rival. Industrial organizations, like empires, pass
through their periods of rise, of eminence and of decline. While the
attribute of a long history of reliable trading is undoubtedly a very
important asset, there are times when changing market conditions create
a demand for a new approach. Smaller, newer, less inhibited firms with
original ideas can often meet this need faster and more effectively than
the elderly giants whose arteries have hardened.

(b) Shortcomings

However impressed you may be with the stability and integrity of
your company—or with its youthfulness and buoyancy—you must
remind yourself that companies, like products, are seldom entirely
superlative. All companies have their shortcomings. If you are unaware
of the shortcomings of your own company before you go out on the
road, you will soon hear about them when you start talking to customers.

We have already touched upon one weakness of some large organizations, the complacency which creeps in when business is obtained a
little too easily, possibly as the result of the lack of any aggressive competition. If complacency does exist within your company, you will
certainly not hear about it from your own management. If they are alive
to its existence, it is axiomatic that they would be dealing with it, and
the problem would disappear. The signs are there to be read and if you
keep your eyes open you can read them as well as the next man. How
often are meetings held to discuss sales policy and performance? How
frequently do members of the management concern themselves with
customers? How informed are they of the reception of the company's
products in the field? How concerned, indeed, are they about this question of complacency? A company whose management has ceased to be
keenly concerned about these questions is coming to the end of its prime
as a competitive force. While it would be entirely wrong to suggest that
all old-established companies are complacent and reactionary, these are
hazards to which they are all potentially liable.

Equally, there are disadvantages for the salesman who represents a
young and vigorous company which is new to the market. The lack of
an established past record will bring doubts to the customer's mind
regarding the reliability of the product and the service which backs it.
A buyer who has been in an industry for many years and has built up
close and friendly relationships with the older-established competitor
will probably be reluctant to take business from his friends and pass
it to a newcomer.

On this question of the possible shortcomings of one's own company,
it is important to bear in mind the past history of the company's

relations with specific customers. The new salesman may find that there is a chequered history with a particular account. There may have been complaints regarding the quality of goods supplied months, or even years, ago. Possibly the service given to an account has been less than satisfactory. There may have been some dispute over prices or credit terms which has left an unsavoury memory in the customer's mind. Find out from your sales management whether there is a back history that you have got to live down. If you know the facts before you introduce yourself to the customer it is so much easier to handle the issue should he raise it with you. As a newcomer, unsullied by your company's past misdeeds, you have the opportunity of wiping the slate clean and making a fresh start.

Another possible shortcoming could be the size of your company's operation. This can be a problem when you try to obtain business with a large-user account. Your firm may be old-established and of undoubted repute. It may, on the other hand, be young, dynamic and enterprising. But if it is small in comparison to its competitors, larger users may express doubts about your ability to satisfy their demands. This question of the available capacity which you have to sell can be vitally important. Customers will wish to know that, should they take business away from their present supplier and pass it to you, your company will be able to provide the quantities of the product which they require for delivery at the required time. If you take an order which oversells your company's capacity to produce within the time-scale required, your customer's production line may stop, with disastrous results for all concerned.

(c) Competitive Merit

Again you must make an assessment and strike a balance between the advantages and the shortcomings of your company, in comparison with those of your competitors, to arrive at a decision regarding its competitive merit in the market. The apparent limitations of a company which is involved in a comparatively small operation can be outweighed by the possession of a more enlightened approach. It may be able to offer a better delivery service simply because its production capacity is not yet fully employed. Conversely the large, established firm, plagued with competition from smaller, very aggressive organizations bent upon obtaining a larger share of the market, may be able to counter with better technical 'know-how' built up over years in the particular industry.

There are other competitive merits. If your manufacturing plant is located within a convenient distance of a particular customer, you will be able to offer a quick delivery service. This will be a particular advantage to the customer in that, in times of emergency, he will be able to call in additional supplies of your product at short notice to meet an unexpected demand. This facility may enable him to work with smaller stocks of the product, so that less of his capital is tied up.

Equally, you may find that your company, though comparatively small in the size of its operation, is more efficiently managed than some of its competitors. This may result in less costly overheads than those of rivals who have large payrolls, occupy costly office blocks and indulge in too much expensive advertising. If your company has this kind of edge on its competitors it may be able to offer keener prices.

Planning Your Sales Drive

The next question which the new salesman should consider before he goes out to meet his customers is how he is going to plan his work. There is a definite need for a planned approach. Generally speaking, when an industrial company appoints a new representative it provides him with a list of user firms, or 'accounts', in his area. These accounts are likely to be spread all over the territory. If the salesman flits around like a busy bee, calling on accounts as his mood takes him, he will waste a great deal of time.

He has to sit down and decide upon a plan which will enable him to cover his territory adequately. Some of his accounts will necessitate calls as often as once a week. Some, once a fortnight. Others, once a month. A few, perhaps, only two or three times a year. The difficulty arises in that they will not be geographically situated to make an arrangement based on visit-frequency convenient. The customer who has to be seen once a week may, in all probability, be located well away from any other customers whose business warrants such frequent attention. Unfortunately, one can only pose the problem, not solve it. It is a problem which arises in every sales area. You will only be able to get to grips with it when you have become fully familiar with the relative importance of your customers and potential customers. In the first instance you should seek the guidance of your sales management and ask for an indication of the call frequency which it expects for all the major users in the territory.

(a) Travelling Time and Calling Time

The question of the allocation of your time is very important. You will be calling on industrial companies to interview fairly senior personnel, such as buyers and works managers. They will not thank you for arriving on their doorstep too early in the morning. If they are works managers, they have got to go round the factory to check that the night-shift ran satisfactorily, that the dayshift has started and all is well, that the plant is running efficiently. They have routine matters to discuss with foremen and chargehands. The buyer, too, has his routine tasks, such as dealing with his post and conferring with subordinates. Many of these duties are dealt with from the time of starting in the morning and occupy those concerned for perhaps an hour, sometimes more. Therefore, the salesman's effective calling time does not start much before 10 a.m. The next closed period is at lunch-time. By late afternoon all the morning's considerations again apply: the works manager must once more check the situation on the shop floor; he has things to see to that he may have been putting off during the day because he has been frequently interrupted, possibly by seeing salesmen such as yourself. The buyer has his mail to sign, his records to attend to. He will not want to see anyone much after 4 p.m. From this, it will be realized that the number of hours in which one can call to see customers is very limited.

When an area is large and there is no concentration of customers in any specific locality, you must consider your travelling time. If, as we have suggested, your first call is made at 10 a.m., and lasts for half an hour, you have then to travel to your next customer. You will in fact be travelling during this already limited calling time. Let us say that your journey lasts half an hour. This will mean that you arrive at your second customer's premises at 11 a.m. If you talk to him for half an hour, it could be midday before you reach your third customer. It can be seen that an average morning's visits are unlikely to exceed three or, at best, four. The prospects after lunch will not be much better. In industrial selling, especially in provincial areas, few salesmen achieve an average of more than six or seven calls a day. When you first start you may be able to do rather more, because customers will probably give you less of their time and the duration of visits will be shorter. Once you are established, however, and the customer and yourself have more to discuss, you will find that the visit which might previously have lasted 20 minutes now stretches to an hour.

If you spend more time than is necessary driving about the countryside, crossing and recrossing your own tracks, you will not get round your territory adequately and your sales to your customers will suffer.

(b) The Allocation of Effort

We have already referred to the list of accounts which will be presented to you by your sales manager naming the firms from which he expects you to obtain business. Some of these accounts will already be buying from your company. Others will be waiting to be developed. These can be described as 'Customers' and 'Potential Customers'. The amount of time which you should devote to calling on each of these groups is difficult to assess in the early stages. There will be certain small established customers, whose business needs less attention from the salesman than a major potential account which has to be worked on. On the other hand, if you spend all your time going after new business, you will turn round one day and find that you have lost to your competitors all the business you started with.

Established customers can occupy a lot of your time if they are to be serviced properly. This balancing of effort between established and potential business will always be a problem and particularly so at the outset when you have no experience to guide you.

Here again, before you go out on the road, discuss this matter in some detail with your sales management. You will find, when you get going, that you will be able to bring your own ideas to the subject and these may not necessarily agree with the assessment of the 'inside' people. Initially, however, these 'inside' people will have greater knowledge than you of the territory and the way it has been run previously.

(c) How To Obtain Appointments

Getting an appointment to go and sell something to somebody is not easy. So far as established customers are concerned, one usually finds that they are quite happy to fit in a visit from a salesman. Indeed, the more enlightened the buyer, the more he will welcome such visits. He wants to see his supplier's representative regularly, to discuss the details of his orders, to take up queries and to learn of any changes which may affect quality, price or service. To get such an appointment it is merely a question of picking up the telephone.

We are not so concerned with appointments with regular customers. Our problem is how to get an appointment with the buyer or works manager of a firm with whom your company is not doing business. From the time your 'prospect' answers the telephone, this is a selling job. You have to give him reasons why he should allow his time to be taken up in seeing you.

It may be unwise to say too much on the telephone. Imagine the telephone conversation as being rather like a 'trailer' at the cinema: if you give away the 'plot' your prospective patron will not bother to see the film! Your task at this stage must be to whet his appetite. When you phone a man for an appointment, quite naturally his first question is going to be: 'What do you want to see me about?' Upon the way you answer that question often stands or falls your chance of gaining an interview. If you merely tell him that you have taken over the area and would like to meet him, you risk inviting a rebuff. If his business is worth having, he is probably a busy man. He is not going to waste time seeing you just to shake hands and exchange pleasantries with a stranger. He will want to know that any time he devotes to seeing you will have some value *to him*. The answer to the question: 'Why do you want to see me?' should be: 'Because we have products which I think you should look at'.

The potential customer may well answer that he already knows your products, that he does not think there is much you can offer him, that he is very busy and cannot spare the time . . . etc.

This is where the conversation becomes difficult. Important buyers have so many approaches made to them by prospecting salesmen that they have no option but to limit the number whom they interview; otherwise, they would never get any other work done. Without wishing to be unpleasant to callers, they simply have to fob off the majority, in order to have time to see the minority whom they consider it important to interview. You must get into that minority list. You will do so only if the reasons you put forward are persuasive. You must put it to the buyer that it is some time since your products were discussed with him; that you have got new products in your range; that your company has done a great deal of development work; and that you believe it is important that he should see for himself what you have to offer, because it can be of value to him. He must be made to feel that he should see you, that he should examine your products again and that by giving you a piece of his time he will not be wasting it.

Here we must delve, for a moment, into the motivations of buyers or those individuals, by any other title, whose responsibility it is to purchase components or raw materials within the client company. The buyer will not last long in his job if he talks only to his current suppliers. His duty, at all times, is to buy as efficiently as possible, to buy not only on price but also on quality and service. Should someone else in his organization come up with the suggestion that they could buy at a keener price, or buy a better product, the buyer who has failed to obtain and check this information for himself will not hold his job for long in a really efficient firm.

Undoubtedly there are firms which tolerate inefficient buyers. However, you must always assume that the buyers with whom you have to deal are on top of their jobs. You may be lucky and find buyers who are quite prepared to see a new face and have a chat with you without having first established that you have anything of interest to tell them. Sooner or later, however, you will be faced with the situation where, by telephone, you must sell the idea that by refusing to see you, a buyer could be missing something of importance. Providing you can do that, you will get your interview.

CHAPTER FIVE

KNOW THE PURPOSE OF YOUR VISIT

In an earlier chapter we discussed the need to prepare yourself before you were interviewed for the job. I said then that the practice of pre-interview preparation would become an essential part of your daily work once you started to call on customers as a sales representative. Just as I asked you to do some hard thinking before you went for your job interview, before you walk into a customer's office you need to think about why you are going there.

Why are you going to see this customer? The short answer is: to sell him the products of your company. It is not, however, as simple as that. Before you can reach the point where you can achieve a sale, there are certain factors which have to be established, certain information which you need to obtain. In this chapter we are going to discuss what those factors are. First of all, however, I want to impress upon you the importance of having clearly defined objectives.

Consider the situation from the customer's point of view. He has agreed to see you. You must assume he is a busy man. He is seeing you because it is part of his job to interview suppliers' representatives in order to keep himself informed of what may be available to his company in the market. In addition to obtaining information, he is also showing courtesy to your company. This, again, is part of his job, for it is a very short-sighted buyer who does not wish to engender goodwill with suppliers, whether he is currently buying from them or not. There are important advantages to the buyer who is on good terms with potential suppliers. The day may come when, for one reason or another, his current supplier is unable to provide the product or the service he requires; he must then turn elsewhere, quickly, to obtain his supplies. If he is already liked and respected by the potential supplier, by the salesman, the sales manager, the technical personnel, he will get that little extra attention, that priority service which is the natural response to a request from a friend as distinct from a mere name on a letterhead. Suppliers' personnel, like customer's personnel, are human. Hence the buyer who has been discourteous to a potential supplier will not get the best service when, in an emergency, he turns to him for urgent supplies. Good buyers know this. They know that, regardless of the volume of business which they have to place, maintaining good relations with all suppliers, current or potential, is an essential insurance.

The buyer, then, will be prepared to devote a reasonable length of time to his interview with you. This might be between ten minutes and half an hour, depending on the value of the conversation to him.

Next, consider this visit from your company's point of view. The visit has a cost attached to it. You can calculate this cost for yourself by adding your salary to your expenses for any given period, a month, a quarter or a half-year, and dividing the total by the number of calls made on customers during that period. The final figure represents the average cost to your company of every call which you make. Every minute you are talking to your customer you are spending so much of your company's money. If you call on a customer without having a clear idea of what you are going to talk about, you will waste not only his time but also your company's money.

This is why clearly defined objectives are important. Let us consider what they are.

Assess the Business which the Customer has to Offer

When one is selling industrial products, it is rare to obtain a sale on a single visit. The client company is usually already engaged in the manufacture of those end-products in which it specializes. This means that it is already consuming a material or a component, or is using a service, similar to that which you have to offer. It is unlikely, therefore, that the buyer is waiting to place an order on the specific occasion of your visit. The exception is where the customer has contacted your company and asked that a representative should call. Normally your visit will be unsolicited and it is you, not the buyer, who is making the approach. The buyer will have to establish a number of factors about your product; its price, its suitability for his process and its availability, before he makes a decision to purchase.

Your first visit will therefore be but one stage in the process of negotiation with this particular customer. There are several factors which both you and he need to know about before the decision to enter into business can be reached. Just as your potential customer must first weigh up the pros and cons of placing business with your company, so you must assess the value to your company of acquiring this customer's business. From your assessment you will be able to decide whether you should pursue this business and how you will go about securing it.

The facts to be established can be summarized as follows:

(*a*) What product(s) does this customer use?
(*b*) How much of the product does he use?
(*c*) How often does he order it?
(*d*) At what price does he expect to buy it?

Going back to the example of the lacquer paint which we introduced in Chapter Four, you will want to establish what kind of paint the customer uses. Does he require a special type or quality? If so, have you a suitable product within your own range? If you have, there is the prospect of some business here. If you have not, it will be necessary to do one of two things: (*a*) persuade your company to produce a paint of suitable quality, or (*b*) explore the possibility of getting the customer to change to a grade within your range.

Next, you must find out how much paint he uses. If his requirements are very small, they may be below the minimum quantities which your company is prepared to supply. Alternatively, if he is a very large user, his demand, if you were to succeed in getting his business, could outstrip your company's ability to supply and you would fail to meet his delivery requirements.

Thirdly, how often does the customer require deliveries? A firm with a large consumption but limited storage facilities may demand frequent deliveries. If they are situated off the beaten track, some special transport arrangements might be necessary to maintain the required service.

Finally, there is the question of price. If the customer is already buying relatively cheaply, can your company compete? At what price would the customer be prepared to purchase your paint? Would he be prepared to pay a higher price for a better product? Alternatively, would he be prepared to accept a slightly lower quality at a lower price?

Before you can assess the value of this customer's business, before you can decide whether it is in the interests of your company that you should devote future calling time to obtain this business, you will need answers to all the above questions.

Assess the Possibilities of Obtaining Business

Having established what it is that the customer buys and the value of the business which he might place with your company, you have next to find out what are the chances of getting this business. It is one of the most important considerations in your preliminary assessment of an account. We discussed earlier the problem of limited calling time and the correct application of effort to obtain sales. Nothing is to be gained by trying to obtain business when it is apparent that the customer has valid reasons for remaining with his current supplier. This is not the counsel of defeatism. All good salesmen are incurable optimists, but some allow their optimism to override reality. You must devote your efforts where there is a likelihood of results. To call every week, month after month, on a particular account, in the vain hope of getting business which is clearly not going to come your way is to throw away the valuable time that could be better spent on less intractable customers.

However, business currently in the hands of competitors is not always as strongly held as might at first glance appear. Suppose that one of the potential customers in your area informs you that he is buying from another supplier on contract. Your initial reaction could be that for a year or so the business is 'tied up'. On that assumption, there would seem little point in pursuing the matter, at least until such time as the contract came up for renewal. But wait a moment! For what quantity has the customer contracted? For what period of time?

Let us take an example. The customer is a yarn manufacturer. He produces x million yards of a certain quality yarn per year, and buys y thousand plastic bobbins per year on which the yarn is wound by high-speed machinery. He has contracted with your competitor for the supply of these bobbins for six months. If, at the time of your visit, the contract has four months to run before renewal, you might assume that you have no chance of selling your bobbins for four months. Further questioning of the customer might, however, establish that he has recently obtained an important piece of additional business, as the result of which he has to put in more plant and extra winding machines. His rate of consumption of bobbins will also increase. This means that he will require more bobbins from your competitor than he originally estimated. The y thousand for which he contracted will be used up, not in six months, but in three. Furthermore, because of his greatly increased usage of bobbins, he may well decide that it would be unwise to have 'all his eggs in one basket'. Prudence may dictate to him the need for a second supplier. The possibilities of obtaining business at this account, which initially looked slim, now appear very much better. Providing you can offer a suitable line of bobbins at the right price and can give him as good a delivery service as he is getting from his present supplier, you may well obtain at least a share of the additional business he has to place.

In assessing opportunities, it should be realized that business seldom changes hands without good cause. If you make a practice of studying the case-histories of accounts in your territory over a period of time, you will come to recognize those factors which lead customers to change their suppliers. There are, in fact, cycles in the history of accounts, when several factors come together and produce an opportunity for a potential supplier to move in and acquire business. These factors all contain one common element, that of change. It may be a change in the customer's needs or a change in the ability of his current supplier to satisfy those needs. The requirements of a customer seldom remain constant over a long period of time. We have discussed previously the changing pattern in the fortunes of industrial organizations, how they rise, reach their prime, and decline. That is one factor. Another is that, to remain competitive in his particular market, the customer must modify his products, extend his range, improve his production. He will be striving always for greater production efficiency, for improvement in product quality and for increased output. At the same time he will be seeking reductions in his raw material costs and the cost of bought-in components.

The current supplier will have to match his customer's progress by improvements to the product which he sells to him. He must also maintain his competitive position on price and service. It is almost inevitable in this constantly moving situation that some unbalance should occur between the demands of the customer and the ability of his current supplier to meet those demands. Naturally enough, the point of unbalance is where the supplier's position is most vulnerable, and that of a potential supplier most promising.

To illustrate this we will return to the case of the customer who uses large quantities of lacquer paint. He has been purchasing his requirements from your competitor over a number of years. The high-gloss properties of his paint, coupled with his keen price and good delivery service, have enabled your competitor to hold this account despite all the efforts of your company and others to break in. However, in order to meet changing demands in his own market, the customer now finds it necessary to coat certain of his products with a matt-finish lacquer. He tells his supplier that he will continue to buy the same total quantity of paint, but in future will require only 70 per cent of his requirements in gloss finish and 30 per cent in matt finish. He asks for samples of matt-finish lacquer to approve the quality.

This might present his supplier with difficulties. It may be that his process is such that he cannot maintain in a matt-finish grade the ease of spraying and speed of drying which have been the main selling features of his gloss paint for many years. Alternatively, while he may be able to make an acceptable matt-finish quality, the quantity the customer requires is insufficient for economic production. He will have to ask for a higher price. Yet again, he may have an acceptable quality matt-finish paint, which he is already producing in bulk at an economic price, but because he is already selling all his output of this quality to other customers, he cannot take on any more business in matt-finish paint until he expands his manufacturing capacity.

It will be seen that any one of these alternative difficulties could place the current supplier in a vulnerable position. The customer *must* find an adequate source of supply for his matt-finish paint. If the difficulties cannot be quickly overcome, he will have to look elsewhere, no matter how much he values his present supplier.

The example illustrates the point that no piece of business, however strongly it may seem to be held by the present supplier, remains unassailable for ever. In assessing the possibilities of obtaining business, you have to consider not only the competitive merits of your own product and your own company, but also the likelihood of change in the requirements of the customer. Where a short-term change is indicated, you may rate your chances of business fairly high and therefore decide to expend a considerable proportion of your time in calling on the account. If, however, the opportunity for business is more likely only in the long term, you may decide that a periodic call, to maintain contact and keep the situation under review, will suffice.

Establish the Customer's Requirements

When you make your first visit to a potential customer, one of your objectives will be to establish in detail exactly what his requirements are. Much subsequent selling effort can be wasted if the real needs of the customer are not fully appreciated at the outset. We have already said that success in industrial selling is very often the marrying of the product to the application. That is why you should seek as full a knowledge as possible of what the customer proposes to do with your product should he decide to buy it.

While many large manufacturing organizations maintain extensive testing laboratories, staffed by highly trained and experienced technical personnel who are able to guide their purchasing departments in the selection of raw materials and bought-in components, the vast majority of small and not-so-small firms rely on their suppliers to submit the right grade to suit their process. This places a heavy responsibility on the supplier and on the supplier's representative. Although you may not be a 'technical salesman' in the sense of having technical qualifications relating to your product, it is important that any technical information you obtain from customers should be as accurate as possible.

Leaving aside technical considerations, the commercial requirements of the customer have to be clearly established. What quantity of the product will the customer use? With what frequency will he require deliveries? What size of deliveries is he prepared to take? The answers to these questions not only establish the value of the potential business to your company, they are also an indication of the amount of service which will be required. The customer who takes a large annual quantity of your product in two deliveries is obviously going to place less strain on your delivery service than one who orders the same overall quantity but requires delivery in small batches once a week.

Some customers may wish to place a bulk forward order to cover their requirements and will expect your company to maintain a *minimum/ maximum stock* aganst which they will call off supplies as required. As soon as the stock reaches the minimum figure, your firm will have to replenish it up to a level not above the maximum figure which has been agreed. This is a system which often works well for the customer but may present difficulties for the supplier, who has to tie up a sum of money permanently in stock reserved solely for the use of one customer. The rate at which this stock is likely to be called off is, therefore, highly relevant to the overall value of the business to your company.

Another customer may require a *consignment stock*. This is a stock of material or goods delivered to his warehouse from which he can draw as and when required. He will be responsible for warehousing the entire quantity at his own expense. He will inform your company when he draws on this stock for his production and your office will send him an invoice for that specific quantity. The customer has the advantage of having the material on his premises, with no hazard of delayed deliveries. Your company, having once delivered the original consignment, has the advantages of an assured sale, a single delivery cost and no warehousing costs. The obvious disadvantage, from the supplier's point of view, is that money is tied up in the consignment stock. Moreover, this stock is servicing only one customer. If the stock were held on the supplier's own premises, he could use it as a general stock to service a number of accounts.

The third consideration in establishing the customer's requirements is the price at which he is prepared to buy. This should not be confused with the price at which he is currently buying a similar product from a competitor. The fact that the price of your product is competitive, i.e. is the same as your competitor's price, does not necessarily mean that it meets your customer's requirements as the price at which he will change suppliers and buy from you. We have said before that price must be a factor in your competitive merit. There are circumstances when price is not the only factor and other considerations such as quality and service may outweigh price in giving you a competitive advantage. But, even where price is the only consideration, merely being competitive may not be enough. In such circumstances, all things, including quality and service, may be equal. Only a keener price may win you the business. It is important to establish this point at an early stage, to prevent wasted time in the pursuit of business which may be currently unattainable simply because you have no leeway on price.

What Your Sales Management Needs to Know—and Why

In addition to selling his company's products, the salesman is also the 'eyes and ears' of his firm within the territory for which he is responsible. In order to control effectively the overall selling operation, the management requires a constant feed-back of information. This should be remembered at every call you make.

The most important information that is required is the state of the trade, whether it is busy, is likely to get busier, or likely to become less busy. Although you may not actually be supplying to a particular customer, if in the course of your conversation he volunteers that he will be using more material, or less material, or about the same amount of material over the next two or three months, this is information of value to your management. From your report and from the reports from other sales areas, the management will gain a broad indication as the months go by of what the market is doing: whether it is expanding, contracting or at a standstill. On the basis of this feed-back of information, it will be possible to plan future levels of production and to decide on the optimum level at which stocks should be held.

The next thing your management needs to know is the activity of competitors. Any snippets of information which you are able to glean about competitors will be useful, not only in assessing your competitive situation with regard to a particular account, but also as a general indication of the policy which your competitors are pursuing in the market. Such information may parallel similar intelligence coming in from other sources and will assist your management in building up a picture.

Which of your competitors is most active at this particular account? How often does the buyer see the competitor's salesman? Is there anything new being offered? These are not questions which should be asked directly; but they should be at the back of your mind when talking to customers. Many buyers are rightly reticent about discussing with one supplier the activities of another. They consider that anything told them by a supplier is confidential. Such a buyer would regard it as 'bad form' if you were to question him regarding his firm's relations with your competitors. This attitude speaks highly of the integrity of the buyer and of his firm and should at all times be respected. On the other hand, many buyers do talk to one supplier about another. When this happens, the best policy is to 'keep your ears open and your mouth shut'. Listen and mentally record, because you may learn much about what your competitors are doing. Do not, however, introduce a discussion about a competitor nor press for more information than is volunteered. To do so would be to run the risk of offending your customer and to put him on his guard in the future. (Certain exceptions to this rule concerning the seeking of information about competitors will be discussed later.)

There are other things which your sales management needs to know and which are specific to calls on individual accounts. If there is the possibility that you could do business with a particular customer, your management will have to decide whether this business is wanted. All the factors we have already considered, the possibility of obtaining business and the establishment of the customer's requirements, play a relevant part in helping the sales management to reach a decision. The quantities the customer can use, the grade he requires, the price which can be obtained, the delivery requirements which the customer will specify, the stock-holding requirements, all these will have to be considered.

Equally, your management will want to know something about the nature of the potential customer's business. If this is the first visit made to the firm in question by you or any other representative of your company for some considerable time, your management will need to know something of the credit-worthiness of this account. Because there is simply no point in selling your product or service to a customer if you are not going to get paid for it, the question of credit-worthiness is going to come up again and again in your career as an industrial salesman.

Until such time as you obtain an order and business commences with a particular customer, his credit-worthiness may not seem important to you. But very often in industrial selling an initial order is placed some time after the representative's visit. It occurs when the buyer reaches the point where he has to re-order. He has remembered what the salesman has told him, has evaluated the samples which have been sent to him, has read the specifications for the product and has decided to place the business with your company. Such an order may be placed by telephone and confirmed later in writing. It is probably placed without the salesman's knowledge, until he rings his office and learns the good news. Meanwhile, the order is under scrutiny at the sales office and the first decision which has to be made is whether or not the goods in question can be supplied on credit. If there is no up-to-date information available on the credit-worthiness of the customer, problems can arise. The customer will have to be asked for trade references. When received, these will have to be taken up and this is a time-consuming process. Recourse may be had to those organizations which specialize in the provision of confidential reports on the credit-worthiness of industrial companies. Here again, time must elapse before the information becomes available. All this while the order, so important to you, to your company and, indeed, to your customer, lies dormant until a decision can be reached.

It is important, therefore, that when you make your first contact with a new account, you should arrive at your own assessment of its credit-worthiness. The term simply means the worthiness of the customer to receive a certain amount of credit, and the limit of that credit will depend upon his ability to pay for the goods which your company may, at some future date, supply to him.

Credit-worthiness assessments are based on confidence. Nobody can be sure that a customer is going to pay his bill, nobody can be sure that the customer's customer is going to pay him for the products which he will process from your material. In the event that he does not get his money from his customer, he may be financially embarrassed and not be able to settle his account with your company. Therefore, knowledge of the substance of your potential customer is of vital interest to your management. They may not need to refer to this information in the early stages, but once they receive an order they will consult their files to bring themselves up to date on the customer. They will note that you have had this or that to say about your assessment of his substance and stability. They may not necessarily take your word for it, but your comments and recommendations will colour their impression of your new customer.

Let us consider some of the factors which contribute to an assessment for credit-worthiness.

(a) Type of Premises

If the firm occupies dirty, back-street premises with the paint peeling off the walls, you might consider that they are not making enough money to be able to expend some of their profits in maintaining the place in a reasonable condition. It could be a fair sign that the profits made are slender, perhaps non-existent. This firm may only just be paying its way.

(b) Number of Persons Employed

This will give you a fair indication of the size of the undertaking and its possible turnover. It is not suggested that a firm with the wrong trading policy, inferior products and misguided sales efforts will avoid bankruptcy simply because it occupies large premises and employs a lot of people. But some idea of its present turnover can be assessed if it is meeting a fairly large payroll every week. A high turnover suggests that sufficient money is employed in the business to conduct it at this level of trading.

(c) Type of Plant

It is useful to try and discover the number and type of machines in use, whether they are new or second-hand, whether fully-owned by the firm or being bought on hire-purchase. In the latter event, the firm's production and future trading could be in jeopardy should it run into financial difficulties and be unable to pay the H.P. premium.

(d) The Identity of the Customer's Customers

If the majority of the customer's work is for companies of limited substance, there is always the hazard that one or other of them may go into liquidation and your customer may not get paid for the work he has done or the goods which he has supplied. If the amount involved is substantial, this could place your customer in serious difficulty and prevent him from settling his account with your company. On the other hand, if your customer is supplying reputable companies, well established in their field, such information will encourage your management to take a greater risk in the amount of credit which it makes available to him.

CHAPTER SIX

HOW TO GET THE INFORMATION YOU REQUIRE

We have considered in some detail the purpose of your visit to a customer or potential customer. In this chapter we shall go one stage further and discuss ways of acquiring the essential information which will enable you to obtain business and represent your company adequately to its customers.

At every stage so far I have emphasized the need for preparation. To borrow from salesmen's jargon, you should always 'do your homework' before you call on a customer. There are times when it may be necessary, and even desirable, to 'play it by ear', but these are exceptional. The greater part of sales work demands, for its success, careful thought and careful planning. The salesman who has taught himself to think ahead and to anticipate questions, unexpected situations or changed circumstances, will obtain and retain more business in the long run than the man who believes in crossing his bridges when he comes to them. The ability to adapt one's approach and to react suitably to unexpected challenges is one of the hallmarks of the good industrial salesman, and the last thing I wish to suggest is that you should never deviate from a planned approach when circumstances demand it. What I do insist, however, is that you should not embark upon your interview with a customer until you have decided on a considered line of approach with specific aims in view.

Having examined in Chapter Five what those aims might be, we shall now consider methods by which they may be achieved.

Whom to Approach in the Client Company

One of the biggest difficulties facing the salesman when he approaches a potential customer for the first time is to know whom to see. Of the members of the client's management whose responsibilities include the interviewing of salesmen, the easiest to see are those who rank lowest in the managerial structure. These are, moreover, the people who may have the least authority to influence the buying policy of the firm. When you call for the first time on an account, you are likely to be interviewed by an assistant buyer or an assistant works manager. If you remain content on subsequent visits always to ask for this individual, you are likely in time to build up a personal relationship with him and this may very well bring you some opportunities for business. However, you may subsequently find that your friendly 'contact', because of his relatively sub-ordinate position, has only limited authority to reach purchasing decisions and it becomes apparent that you will have to establish a connection at a higher level. It is at this stage that you may run into personality problems.

No one likes to feel that he is being passed over. You may very well upset your relationship with your existing 'contact' if you attempt to go over his head to the chief buyer, the works manager, or a director of the company. That is why it is preferable to make contact at the outset with the highest possible level in the client company. If you are able to build up a good personal relationship with a senior member of the management, this need not prevent you from creating good connections with his subordinates. The fact that you are well received by his boss will at least encourage the junior man to show you reasonable deference. Resentment occurs when the salesman makes the mistake of courting the friendship of the subordinate and appearing, suddenly, to repudiate this in favour of a more important 'contact'. Naturally, such ineptitude causes offence and, common courtesy apart, no salesman can afford to offend anyone within a client company.

At an early stage in your calls on a potential customer, therefore, you should make up your mind who is your best 'contact'. Of course one has to be sensible about this. There have been cases of tyro salesmen, having been told that it is best to make contact at the highest possible level, going into a large organization and asking to see the chairman or the managing director. Such a request would, of course, be greeted with derision, and the only impression these salesmen could have made on the staff was that they were very, very inexperienced. The supposed 'rule' that one should deal with the men at the top has to be interpreted realistically and applied with common sense.

There are certain factors to consider before you can decide at what level you want to make contact. Ideally, you will want to be seen by the person who makes the purchasing decisions for the type of product which you are offering. In many medium-sized and large firms the job of purchasing is in the hands of a department. The head of the department, who may be styled the Chief Buyer, the Chief Purchasing Officer, or the Purchasing Manager, will delegate areas of responsibility among his staff according to the amount of money spent annually on certain products. Those classes of goods which represent only a small part of his purchasing budget will be delegated, whereas the major items he will probably handle himself.

If your product constitutes a major item of purchase for the firm in question, it will be correct for you to make contact with the head of purchasing. Alternatively, if it is one which is not a major purchase item for that particular customer, you will want to make contact with whoever has been given the delegated responsibility for buying it. For example, in an organization which makes radio sets, the major items of purchase might be electrical components and plastic cabinets. These are likely to be handled by the chief buyer. Such items as cartons and labels might well be delegated to an assistant buyer. If you are offering cartons to this firm, although you may initially see the chief buyer, he will pass you over to his assistant, who specializes in carton purchases. On subsequent visits there will be no purpose in your attempting to see the chief buyer. You will have to concentrate your attention on the man who is directly concerned with your type of merchandise.

On the other hand, if you are offering electrical components which represent a very large item in the purchasing budget, you may find yourself being received by one of the assistant buyers who has been deputed to interview representatives from potential suppliers. You will discover that this assistant is not in a position to make the ultimate purchasing decisions. You have to get past him, to his boss, if you hope to do business with this account.

There is no doubt that this question of finding out who is the right 'contact' is not an easy one to answer. Even experienced salesmen meet this problem when taking over new accounts. After a few calls, when they have acquired some knowledge of the client company, they realize that the man they have been seeing is unable to give them all the information they want and is not in a position to influence buying strategy in favour of their product. It is then that they decide to establish a different contact. The experienced salesman knows that he has to reach this decision before too many calls have taken place. He knows that if he delays and establishes too close a connection with his present contact, he is going to upset him when he goes over his head. Once he realizes his mistake, he very quickly 'switches horses' and makes a point of seeing only the man who really matters. If necessary, he will refrain from calling at the particular account unless he has an appointment with the senior individual.

When you are starting out in your territory, you will probably be given a list of names of known contacts within client companies. Initially, you should ask for these people and during your conversation try to discover the names of other members of the management and their functions. You will have to weigh up, in your own mind, whether the person to whom you are speaking does in fact have adequate purchasing responsibility for your product. If, for example, you know that the firm buys several thousand pounds' worth of your type of product every year, ask yourself whether it is likely that the person you are seeing has been given that degree of responsibility. If he is a very young man, you may decide that he is an assistant who has been sent by the chief buyer to see what you want and to get rid of you. Bear in mind that substantial firms seldom place heavy buying responsibility upon young and inexperienced personnel.

Very often, junior members of the buying staff like to give the impression to salesmen that they are the people to deal with. This results from a natural desire to seem important. Also, junior buyers are, quite rightly, anxious to establish personal connections with potential suppliers against the day when they have to make purchasing decisions of their own. Meanwhile, the senior buyer, because he has so many other tasks to deal with and because he must spend a high proportion of his time with the senior representatives of important supplier companies, will delegate to his juniors the job of seeing salesmen from those companies who are not currently important to him.

Among the difficulties of calling on a firm for the first time, is that you may have no 'contact' and do not know the name of an individual for whom to ask. Some young salesmen turn up at the reception desk and say: 'I would like to see your buyer, please'. This immediately announces to the receptionists or commissionaire that here is a representative who has never called before, probably knows little or nothing about the firm and its requirements and may well be going to waste the time of the buyer or manager who sees him. When they speak on the internal telephone to that person and say 'Mr. Bloggs of the Such and Such Company is in Reception and asks to see the buyer', the buyer, too, will get much the same impression. Before he has met you and had a chance of sizing you up, he will probably decide that this is just a chance call on your part and may think it hardly worth while interrupting his other work in order to see you.

Before you call on a new potential customer, therefore, you should try and get the name of at least one individual in the firm. This can sometimes be done by making a casual inquiry of another customer in the same trade. Most buyers know the identity of their opposite numbers dealing with similar products in other firms and there is nothing to prevent your putting the occasional question to a friendly contact about the names of people in other companies. Most people are willing to help a young salesman with what is, to them, commonplace information. But do not burden your contact with a list of queries; this would be an imposition. The casual question, however, will usually extract a few leads which will enable you to make initial contact with other firms. You should at all times keep your ears open for names when conversing with your customers. The discovery of contacts in the various trades and industries which may use your product is vitally important to your success in industrial selling.

There is one other point which is worth remembering on this question of contacts. You can never have too many friends within the client company. Do not be the kind of salesman who 'switches on' only when he is face to face with the buyer or someone he thinks is going to do him some good. Everybody in the client company can do you some good and they can do you some harm, too, if they do not like you. Experienced salesmen know that the receptionist must at all times be treated with courtesy. She can often be helpful, especially when her boss is elusive. Treat her in a friendly fashion, but avoid any attempt at mild flirtation, which will only provoke embarrassment and is hardly conducive to the respect and liking which must at all times be your objective when dealing with your customers' staff. If the man you want to interview sends out a message that he cannot see you, do not try to get the girl or the gate-keeper to go back and argue your case for you. Do not make their jobs more difficult for them.

On the other hand, being pleasant, polite and prepared to make small talk while waiting to be seen, helps to create a friendly relationship. You are likely to meet these 'front-of-house' people very regularly over the months and years to come. If they like you as an individual, they will always do the best they can to help you, consistent with their duty to their company. Instead of merely saying: 'Mr. Smith is not in his office and cannot be contacted', the receptionist may well suggest: 'As Mr. Brown is free you may like to see him first', while she puts out a Tannoy call for Mr. Smith. Again, when you have called without an appointment and have just missed your contact, she may say: 'He has only popped out for about half an hour. If you like to fit in another call in the district, I'll tell him you're coming back, then perhaps he will not go to lunch until he's seen you'. Such episodes may seem trivial. But it is the trivialities which make or mar the working day and the salesman who has made friends along his way can work not only more pleasantly, but also more efficiently.

How to Introduce Yourself and Your Company

Now that you have obtained the interview, having been received by your contact, how should you introduce yourself?

Until you have become known personally to your customer, it is your company, rather than you as an individual, in which he is interested. He has been prepared to see you not because he is interested in John Smith, Sales Representative, but because he wishes to learn what the XYZ Company may have to offer him. Let him know who you are and what your position is with your company: 'Good morning, Mr. Brown. My name is John Smith. I am representing the XYZ Company and have recently been appointed to this area'. That is enough about you for the present. Do not, at this stage, bore him with a potted biography of your past career, your hopes and ambitions. He is unlikely to be interested. Get on with the subject in which he *is* interested, the products or services which you have to offer. 'We are manufacturers of synthetic lacquer finishes . . .' Ask him if he knows anything about your firm. If not, or if he has only a vague idea, explain in a few words the company story. 'Our factory and head office is at Barchester. We have a capacity of about n thousand gallons, which puts us half-way between our largest and our smallest competitors. It is a fairly new plant, built only seven years ago. We have been going since 1954 and are still expanding. Next year we expect to complete our expansion programme with a new factory of about 20,000 square feet at Oxbridge . . .'

It is at this stage that you must remember your company's competitive merit. The customer will be weighing up in his mind whether yours is a company with which he might conceivably do business at some future time, so you should now stress these merits. Stress your firm's attributes, then overcome any thoughts the customer might have regarding its limitations by stating them frankly. Subsequently, point out that these limitations are outweighed by the special attributes which you believe make your firm a suitable supplier, so far as his requirements are concerned. 'It is, of course, true that we are one of the smaller firms in the industry, Mr Brown. We are not as well known as the Elephantine Company or Colossal Giants Ltd., but this does give us certain advantages, particularly when we are dealing with a company such as yours, which may require "specials". We often find that customers come to us because they cannot get special qualities made up for them elsewhere, and this is where we score. I suppose you could say that we specialize in "specials" . . .'

This introductory sequence is important to your purpose, not only because you are able to put over part of your 'message', which is to boost your company, but it also gives the buyer the chance to 'size you up' as a person. Negotiation for business in the industrial field is, as we have said before, a lengthy process. Just as you have to unfold the story about your company, so the buyer must be prepared to tell you what his firm makes, what are its leading products, its methods of manufacture and the types and quantities of materials or components which it buys. Such information, while not highly secret, is to some extent confidential. The buyer will not discuss such details with a stranger unless he considers it necessary to do so. As you explain who, what and where your company stands in the market, he will begin to fit it into a category. Perhaps your firm has been operating for several years but has concentrated on products which this customer does not use. Now you have extended your range to include items which could be of interest to him. This will explain to him why he has not been approached by your company before. It will also register in his mind that your established position in other fields marks your company as one which is successful and therefore competitive. If it is already well established, it is unlikely to have embarked on a new range of products without having first made sure that they will meet the demands of the market.

This is very much conjecture and also very much in the future but at this early stage in the conversation the message will have got across to him that here is an interesting new potential supplier, who may have something of advantage to offer him.

It also provides you with the opportunity to project yourself. The way you talk about your company, the way you express yourself, gives the buyer the chance to assess the type of man he is dealing with. It is a common experience to be never quite sure of a stranger. At the moment you pass through the doorway into his office you are a stranger. After the few minutes during which you have been speaking, he begins to see you as a personality. Remember that personality has to be projected by speech. The person who hardly opens his mouth discloses nothing of himself, remains a stranger and, therefore, someone of whom to beware.

We discussed earlier the possible hazard of an unfortunate past history at certain accounts. There may, in fact, be something in your company's past dealings with this particular customer which has to be lived down. Alternatively, the buyer may have some prejudice against your firm, not as the result of personal experience, but from talk he has heard in the trade. Such things happen. Companies get labels attached to them as being, for example, price-cutters, or bad on service, or offering products variable in quality. While originally there may have been substance to such reputations, often the disparaging label still sticks long after the failing has been put right. It is at this early stage in your interview that the customer who harbours such doubts about your company is likely to reveal them.

It is important that he should do so and that you should be aware of the problem before you enter into a discussion of your product. We have already alluded to the need of knowing the limitations of your company before you start. If the customer does hold a prejudiced view of your firm, now is the time to bring it into the open and deal with it.

Another factor is that this discussion of your company will provide an opportunity for the customer to disclose, albeit unintentionally, his attitude to your competitive merit. 'Yes, but we normally only deal with the bigger firms', or 'These large firms are all alike. They don't want to deal with people like us because we cannot take delivery in large enough quantities', or 'We used to put all our business with Super Colossal. They're very nice people, but their service got so bad . . . Well, I suppose now that they have been bought out by International Giants they don't think our business big enough to worry about . . .' or yet again, 'We buy mostly from the Elephantine Company. You can't touch them when it comes to quality. Of course, they're a bit slow like all these big firms, and their delivery is lengthy. But they're very nice people to do business with. The slightest thing that goes wrong and they come and see us and put it right with never an argument.' Such revealing remarks at the outset of your interview are manna from Heaven to the salesman who wants to know 'how the wind blows' at a new account.

Maintain an Orderly Sequence of Inquiries

In Chapter Five we spoke of the importance of clearly defined objectives. We have also touched upon the limited amount of calling time available to the industrial salesman and the limited duration of visits. If you are to get the maximum value out of your initial call on a potential customer, you must extract as much information as possible upon which to base your future selling approach.

Providing you have followed the precepts already discussed, you will approach your customer with several specific questions to which you require answers. With experience and practice, these leading questions will come to you automatically as the conversation develops. In the early stages, however, it is advisable to have a mental list of the points you wish to raise and to raise them in an orderly sequence. You can then tick them off in your mind as you deal with them. At the end of the interview you will know that you have covered them all and thus avoid the disconcerting doubt that you may have forgotten something. There is nothing more frustrating than to bid your customer farewell, get into your car and, half a mile down the road, remember something that you should have asked him. Even experienced salesmen, who should know better, on occasion have to give themselves a mental kick because they have forgotten to raise a particular point and realize they have only got half the story.

There is another reason why an orderly sequence of inquiries is important. You may not, at first, remember all that the customer tells you. Conversation seldom follows a definite pattern, and the information you receive will probably be imparted to you in a jumbled manner. If you have a sequence of questions firmly established in your mind, it is easier to relate the answers to them; they are also more likely to remain fresh in your mind than if you have nothing with which to 'key' them.

Finally, an orderly sequence of questions is indicative of an orderly mind and a professional approach. The customer to whom you are talking is a business man, and he is bound to appreciate the fact that you have given some forethought to the interview and have conducted it in a business-like way. Such an impression will go a long way to encourage the customer to see you on your next visit. He will know that you are a man with a purpose and not one of those time-wasting callers who muddle from one subject to another and whose sole objective appears to be nothing more than a report to their superiors that they have 'called there'.

Ways and Means of Extracting Information from Your Customers

Generally speaking, you will find that most buyers are prepared to answer your queries about their requirements, the quantities they order, the grade or quality in which they are interested and the kind of deliveries they normally expect. However, buyers do not always wish to reveal to potential suppliers certain things which you and your company need to know, before you can decide your best method of approach. In the main, the information which they may not wish to divulge will concern the competitive position of their current supplier, or offers which they have received from other contenders for their business.

I have already cautioned you about the danger of appearing to pry into the activities of your competitors. This rule still holds good. You must at all times remember that the good buyer will regard his arrangements with your competitor as confidential, just as you will expect that your discussions with him will remain in confidence. To pry into such matters for no relevant purpose will, at the least, appear discourteous. At worst, it may be taken as a sign of disrespect for the buyer's integrity that you should presume him capable of breaking such confidences.

There are times, however, when it may be of paramount importance to your work to know the competition you have to face. You will need to know the identity of the company with whom you are in competition. We have already said that success in industrial selling often results from the marrying of the product to the application. Where an application is already in being, utilizing a competitive material or component, you will need to identify that product. You will need to know the grade or quality which the competitor is currently supplying in order to decide, on the basis of competitive merit, the grade or quality of your own product which must be offered to compete for the business. It may not be enough to offer your best grade, because your best grade may be too expensive. The competitor who holds the business has established a grade, not necessarily his best or his worst, which suits the application technically and falls within a price bracket appropriate to the economics of the job. He may have made several attempts, putting up several samples on a trial-and-error basis, before he got the business.

If the job started on his product, the customer may well have tolerated a number of trials to establish the right material for his particular purpose. Now that the job is in production, however, he will be less tolerant to a potential supplier. Trials of a new material are much more disruptive when a job is already in production than during the development stage. The personnel in the shop responsible for reaching output targets will be reluctant to break into a run to test a sample. They will do so occasionally if their purchasing department requests it, on the grounds that they wish to consider an alternative source of supply which may offer technical or economic advantage. But a buyer will not wish to interrupt production to evaluate a range of such samples. Therefore, you must hit the target first time if you can. The obvious way to do this is to know the grade currently in use and to offer your nearest alternative, which you believe may show the requisite technical or commercial advantage.

It is possible that if you ask the customer outright who his current supplier is he will tell you. On the other hand he may say that he does not wish to tell you. When you report back to your sales manager that the customer will not divulge the identity of his current supplier, he can hardly censure you, but he may well think that you have accepted the rebuff too easily. Negative information, in this instance, is useless. You will be expected at least to narrow the field of possibilities. If you are able to report back that, in your opinion, the supplier is unlikely to be this, that or the other company, but could be one of two or three others, and give your reasons for this opinion, both you and your sales manager will have something to work on. With his greater knowledge of the market, and the information he is getting from other sales areas, it is possible that the sales manager can, by a process of elimination, deduce the identity of the competitor in question.

How then, do you go about narrowing the field? To do so, you need to know something about your competitors: who they are, the class of trade in which they are most active and the nature and special properties of their products.

From what the customer has volunteered about the requirements of the job, you may be able to deduce that only certain of your competitors are among those likely to be supplying. Providing you have a good knowledge of the policies and products of these firms, it will be possible to eliminate further by judicious questioning. It is rather like the parlour game 'Twenty Questions', except that you will not get anything like 20 answers from your prospective customer. If you have ever played this game, you will know that the secret is to ask certain general questions where even a negative answer is a guide and enables the player to either include or eliminate areas of probability.

This may strike you as a rather childish way of going about your business. You must remember, however, that business really is a game. It is a game, not of chance, but of wits. Considerable stakes may be involved in the outcome and it is your duty to do all you can to obtain the information which your company needs.

Long experience of dealing with buyers in the industrial field indicates that one is seldom told a deliberate lie. But buyers often show considerable skill in evading a direct answer when it suits them to do so, and the salesman needs to be equally skilled to meet and overcome this opposition. The competent salesman therefore cultivates the art of elimination. Elimination is an accepted device of industrial negotiation. It involves no betrayal of confidential information, so the salesman can establish his facts without offending the buyer's integrity.

The Art of 'Trailing Your Cloak'

Another method which practised salesmen employ is sometimes called for want of a better name, 'trailing one's cloak'. The phrase is borrowed from the jargon of the bull-ring, where the matador literally trails his cloak before the bull to test the beast's reactions. Cloak-trailing in industrial negotiation is the device of suggesting a possible line of approach, without any implication of commitment, to gauge the buyer's reaction. The main use of this stratagem occurs during discussions concerning price.

Often one is faced with the problem of establishing the price at which business may be gained. Where a large contract is at stake, the buyer may decide not to guide the salesman on the price he should quote. He will hope that, being eager to obtain the business and being unaware of what his competitors may already have quoted, the salesman will offer a very low figure. It is the buyer's duty to seek the lowest possible price. It is your duty, as the seller, to get the highest possible price commensurate with landing the order.

You will obviously not want to quote too low; profit margins for most industrial products sold in a highly competitive market may already be slender. You will be expected by your company to get the best price possible. Your customer, however, will tell you that you will only get his business if the price you quote is attractive, which means that it must be lower than the price at which he can buy from your competitors. If you do not know the competitor's price, how can you resolve this problem?

If you quote a price which subsequently proves to be lower than necessary to obtain the business, it is not usually possible to retract, for you will have committed yourself and your company. Nor can you start with the highest possible price and work downwards a unit at a time: this would tell an astute buyer that you know little about the market. It might imply that you were desperate to obtain his business and this could encourage the buyer to keep forcing you down until you arrived at an absurdly low figure, one which your company might have to repudiate. Such an outcome would be disastrous.

The better way out of this difficulty is to 'trail your cloak', to suggest to the buyer a price area and, without having committed yourself, gauge his reaction.

Let me illustrate the point with a very hypothetical example, based on an entirely fictional nightmare experienced by an over-worked salesman in building materials.

SHEIKH (*casting his eyes over the expanse of desert*): 'Yes, I could be interested in buying your fine-grain sand, Mr. Jones. What is your price?'

JONES: 'In ten-ton loads, Your Highness, my price is £40 a ton.'

SHEIKH (*deprecatingly*): 'Oh, come now, Mr. Jones! I am already buying below that figure and my present supplier gives me very good service, with regular weekly deliveries. I would only consider changing my source of supply if there was a definite price advantage. You will have to think again.'

JONES (*blandly*): 'Yes, I suppose that with the quantities you use in the desert, you probably are buying very keenly. But still, production costs being what they are these days, I wouldn't have thought that it would pay anyone to ship sand, even in 20-ton loads, at much below £30 to £35 a ton.'

SHEIKH: 'There are plenty of people offering me sand at around those prices.'

JONES (*with a frown*): 'Yes, but I thought you were talking about fine-grain quality, Highness. We all know there is plenty of mixed-grain going cheap. But for a desert of your quality, I wouldn't have thought you would consider that sort of stuff. Frankly, at £30 a ton for fine-grain, it just would not pay me to supply you.'

SHEIKH (*meditating*): 'No, I'm not suggesting I can get *fine*-grain sand at that price. But I'm buying below £40 a ton.'

JONES: 'I suppose that for 20-ton deliveries, against a bulk contract, it is just possible that you can.'

SHEIKH: 'After all, by the time I've paid my tribesmen to spread it all over the desert, my business could not stand £40 a ton.'

JONES (*sympathetically*): 'I can see that. Well, I might be able to drop to, say, £35, providing you can give me a bulk contract.'

SHEIKH (*poker-faced*): I only buy on contract, of course. £35 a ton might be interesting.'

JONES: 'What quantity would you contract for?'

SHEIKH: Well, suppose we say 100 tons?'

JONES: 'A week?'

SHEIKH (*with a laugh*): 'A week? Oh no! A month, of course.'

JONES (*with dismay*): 'I'm sorry. I thought you used much more than that.'

SHEIKH (*spreading his hands*): 'My business is growing. By the end of the year we shall probably be able to talk about that sort of quantity. But not just at present.'

JONES: 'This makes it difficult. I doubt whether my company would be interested in offering a special price for only 100 tons a month. It wouldn't really pay us, you see.'

SHEIKH (*coldly and with apparent loss of interest*): 'Well, it's up to you, Mr. Jones. The business is there. And it's growing. Within the next two or three years we hope to extend our desert right out into the sea.'

JONES: (*after pausing for thought*): 'Well, I'll tell you what I'll do. I might be able to get my people to confirm a price of £37 a ton, for delivery in 20-ton loads to your oasis, providing you give me a contract for 600 tons to be taken over a period not exceeding six months.'

SHEIKH: 'You're not giving anything away, Mr. Jones. However, it does show me a marginal advantage. You'd better come into my tent . . .'

At this point the unfortunate Mr. Jones probably woke up! However, this excerpt does illustrate the point we have been making. From a list price of £40, Jones led the discussion round to what he knew was the semi-ridiculous price of £30. Having established that this was a ridiculous price for the quality under discussion, he worked upwards, without committing himself to a definite offer, until it became apparent that the sheikh did not expect a price as low as £35. He knew that £35 would have got him the business, because his customer showed the first sign of interest when he mentioned that price. By introducing the question of the quantity he would expect to supply at that price, he quickly established two facts: that his customer would be prepared to place a contract for 100 tons per month; secondly, that £35 was not the highest price he could go to. The sheikh merely insisted that he was buying better than £40 a ton. Jones therefore knew that the right price to quote lay somewhere between £39 and £35. He quoted £37, knowing he would get the business.

CHAPTER SEVEN

ASPECTS OF INTERVIEWING

The interviewing of customers is the most interesting aspect of the salesman's work and the most demanding. It demands a rare quality, the ability to understand other people. Instead of the usual cliché that the good salesman is a good psychologist, it is more true to say that the best salesmen never take for granted their ability to understand the motivations of their customers. They know that no two customers are alike and that they must modify their approach in accordance with the personality and temperament of every client who is interviewed.

The Correct Mental Approach

One of the major differences between the work of the retail salesman and the industrial salesman is that the former is dealing with the general public, the majority of whom are likely to have little or no commercial experience, whereas the industrial salesman is dealing with businessmen. He has to sell to professionals and it is important that he should adopt a professional approach to his job.

Let me define what I mean by professionalism. I am asking that you should look upon your work as a sales representative as a professional activity. To achieve success as a salesman it is sometimes necessary to subordinate self in the interests of the job. This subordination of one's private, personal ego has to be maintained throughout your selling activities. Looked at from this aspect, the role of the sales representative is not dissimilar to that of the doctor, the barrister, the school-teacher or the professional entertainer. All such persons are engaged in professional activity and all, to be successful in their chosen sphere, must adopt and maintain a 'public face' in the conduct of their professional duties. Thus the salesman is 'on parade' all the time he is working, that is to say all the time he is in contact with customers.

This principle is easy to forget, especially when you have achieved a measure of friendship with certain customers. The mask of professionalism has a way of slipping when what is, in fact, no more than a good business relationship takes on the appearance of a personal friendship. It may be an exaggeration to claim that there are no personal friendships in business. They are, however, rare. Those little inoffensive liberties which one may feel it is reasonable to take with our personal friends can easily be considered offensive if taken with one's apparently friendly customers.

A friendly relationship between buyer and seller is based, primarily, not on mutual personal regard but on mutual self-interest. The salesman makes a friend of the buyer because he hopes to sell to him. The buyer makes a friend of the salesman because it makes easier the personal contact involved in doing business with him. No doubt many buyers and many salesmen will shake their heads vigorously at these harsh words. They may with justice argue that, frequently, close personal regard and understanding mature from their business relationships. This is true and it is often to the advantage of their respective firms that such close liaison should exist. Nevertheless, the basis of the relationship is a mutual interest in business and, in the majority of cases, this remains the predominant motive.

In one's private friendships, there is an understood, if unspoken, mutual obligation of loyalty. In the friendship which exists between a salesman and his customer, however, there can be no absolute loyalty. This is because both parties have a first loyalty to their employers, whose interests it is their duty to place first at all times. I stress this point because there is a generally held view that the successful sales representative is one who can make close friends of his customers. By all means aim to establish good relations with your clients, but do not delude yourself that the ability to make friends is a primary quality in a salesman.

We all know the type of person who 'likes to meet people'. Generally speaking, the man who 'likes meeting people' likes to be liked. Very often he has a dominant desire and need to be liked. While it is obvious that few of us like being disliked, an obsession with popularity can be a serious handicap for the industrial salesman. There are occasions when he must be prepared to forego some popularity in order to safeguard the interests of his company.

The adoption of a professional approach to your job will ensure that you do not lose sight of the purpose for which you are employed: to create and maintain profitable business for your company. The job requires of you much more than merely establishing friendly relationships with your customers. There are times when the salesman becomes entangled in less pleasant activities, when he has to investigate a complaint or is involved in a dispute over quality, or service, or an account problem. On such occasions, in order to maintain the interests of his company, he may find himself in opposition to his customer. The man who has created too close a bond of personal friendship with his client will find it much harder to accomplish such tasks. But the real danger in such a situation is that the customer who has become a close friend may interpret the salesman's apparent change of allegiance as a betrayal and distrust him in the future.

The importance of the professional approach lies in its detachment. The salesman cannot afford to wear his heart on his sleeve. By this I mean that he must keep his emotions out of his job. He must be capable of hiding his inner feelings. Undoubtedly, there will be many customers whom you will like as individuals. Inevitably, however, there will be some whom you will dislike. You will encounter bores and bullies, people who, for one reason or another, will strike you as objectionable in outlook or behaviour. Very few of your customers will be saints. You will have to learn to take them as they come. Your job is to promote business with them and your likes and dislikes do not come into it. When things go wrong you must be prepared to stand up to abuse, which may be directed both at your company and at yourself. It will be part of your job to take the 'kicks' from irate customers and you will not be at liberty to give as good as you get, not, that is, if you hope to do future business with those accounts.

The quality known as 'good manners' appears to be out-moded in many walks of life today; for the successful salesman, however, it remains an essential attribute. Correct behaviour is never misplaced, regardless of the varying behaviour patterns of one's customers. The image of the old-time commercial traveller, with his crude humour and brash approach is certainly out-moded today. The increasing degree of sophistication one finds among modern industrial management demands that today's sales representative shall be an educated and articulate person, conditioned to behaving at all times in a responsible manner. He is the ambassador of his firm and the image which he displays in his attitude to his customers is an extension of the desired image of his company.

Never embarrass your customer. Do not put him in the position where he has to lose face. No doubt, if you do your job successfully, there will be times when you will succeed in outwitting your customer. This is part of the cut and thrust of business life. Resist the temptation to crow over your success. Let the customer judge for himself that you have won that round. Never force him to look stupid or inefficient. In so doing you will achieve nothing but self-satisfaction and he will neither like you nor respect you for it.

Never wittingly sell a man something he does not want. The short-term gain will be a long-term loss because the customer will make sure that you do not catch him twice. Sharp practice of any kind is not in accord with responsible salesmanship. It will bring both you and your company into disrepute.

In your conversation with customers remember the two great taboos, religion and politics. General conversation between business people frequently includes the discussion of public affairs. Matters relating to national and international politics and other controversial subjects such as race relations and religious persuasion are bound to come up. The salesman must be wary of the extent to which he airs his personal views on such matters. The safest course is to avoid controversial topics. Where the subject is introduced by the customer and your opinions are sought, the greatest diplomacy should be exercised in your response.

Always try to be punctual in keeping your appointments with customers. Nothing gives such a bad impression as to arrive late. There is really no excuse for doing so if you plan your visits properly, making adequate provision for the duration of calls and for intermediate travelling time. To arrive late is to dislocate the buyer's time schedule. It is discourteous and reflects adversely upon your own and your company's reliability. There are, however, two sides to the coin. Providing you that have arrived at your customer's premises punctually, there is no excuse for him to keep you waiting beyond a reasonable length of time. The customer who keeps you 'cooling your heels' in an ante-room for half an hour is not only disrupting your time schedule but, by making you late for your next call, is going to upset your next customer's arrangements. If the buyer has not sent for you within 15 minutes of the announcement of your arrival, you are at liberty to ask the receptionist to give him a gentle reminder.

Always be prepared to let your customer have the last word. If he seems to want it, let him have the last laugh. Do not try to cap his jokes or cramp his style. Never take away the customer's self-esteem, just his order.

In many of the smaller firms, the man you will interview may be a director or the proprietor of the business. It is likely that, in addition to buying components and raw materials, he will handle also the selling side of his business. He, too, will be a professional salesman and will therefore recognize and appreciate your professional approach to your work.

Always display a good opinion of your company, your product and of yourself. Do not seek to confide your personal problems and frustrations to your customer: he will have enough of his own without wishing to hear about yours. Never run down the people within your company. Such disloyalty will immediately reduce the customer's respect.

I have said that one must try to understand the customer's motivation. The subtle way of selling industrial products is to know what is important to each individual customer and to ensure that you guide him for his own good, providing it is not contrary to the interests of your own company. The highest point of achievement one can reach in one's relations with a customer is to become, as it were, his guide, philosopher and friend, the man to whom he turns instinctively when he wants information or advice regarding anything to do with supplies of materials or components. It does not matter that the salesman may not know the answers to all his questions. What does matter is that the customer knows that the salesman can and will find out the answers and that, in providing such information, he will not mislead him. Such assistance can often be given with regard to products one does not oneself handle. There may be no direct profit to your company, but you will have done your customer a service and this helps to build up a bank of goodwill.

Remember that your dealings with each customer must be treated, always, as confidential. The salesman who talks to one of his customers about another is announcing that he cannot be trusted to keep confidences. He will soon find that he is told nothing that his customers do not wish their competitors to know. In Industrial selling there are no geographical boundaries outside which it is safe to talk to one customer about another. A customer in, say, the South of England may well be in fierce competition with a company in Scotland which manufactures an almost identical product destined for the same market.

The Need to Control the Conversation

Having obtained his interview with his prospective customer, the salesman must ensure that he retains the initiative and controls the subsequent conversation. Once again I draw your attention to the two major limitations under which you have to work, the limited number of calls you can make in a day and the limited duration of those calls. It is no exaggeration to say that every minute of your interviewing time is precious and must be made to work for you.

To control the conversation, it is necessary to apply the professional approach we have already discussed. You will be going to your interview with a series of intentions: gaining specific information regarding the customer's requirements, the nature of his business and the activities of your competitors; pressing him to consider your product; obtaining an order. The importance of an orderly approach has already been discussed, but your attempts to proceed along orderly lines and to unfold your story logically, introducing first your company and then your product, will be frustrated if you lose control of the conversation. Should control pass to the customer, you may find your approach disrupted and disorganized. Indeed, it is easy to become so preoccupied in responding to the customers' questions that you lose the opportunity to establish the essential information you require, and your carefully planned approach becomes a shambles.

In certain circumstances, lack of control of the conversation can result in a deterioration of the discussion into an aimless exchange of past experiences. Though tolerably interesting as a means of passing the time, small talk has nothing to do with the purpose of your visit. This can be one of the worst problems facing a young and inexperienced salesman. Some people love the sound of their own voices and you are bound to come across a few customers with this tendency. They will insist on recounting a series of anecdotes based on events and personalities of which you may know nothing and care even less. Desperately, you may find yourself trying to break into the torrent of verbiage long enough to say your piece and then escape. Be consoled that you are not the only sufferer, for all salesmen have experienced crashing bores. They are one of the hazards of the profession. On such occasions the principle to bear in mind is that you are a professional and have a job of work to do. However pleasant or unpleasant the situation may be, as you sit in the customer's office listening to one of his favourite monologues, you are not doing the job you are being paid to do.

In these circumstances the novice may find it difficult to assert himself. As a professional salesman, however, you can only afford to take a certain amount of this treatment. The longer you leave it before you regain control of the conversation, the more difficult it is to do so.

The ebullient buyer who tries to monopolize the conversation needs firm handling. Having been granted an interview, you have a right to be heard. You must persist, in spite of any attempts he may make to change the subject to get you off a difficult point. Such firmness, always providing it is applied in a polite and correct manner, will eventually prevail.

You should never let a customer 'rattle' you by forcing you into a defensive position. This should not happen if you have done your homework correctly, by collecting your facts and planning in advance the points you wish to discuss. If the customer throws at you questions to which you do not have the answer, admit frankly that you do not know but will find out. He is much more likely to respect your honesty and strength of character than if you flounder and invent answers which are obviously based on uncertain knowledge.

The Buyer's Temperament

The novice salesman may be forgiven if, after a day in which he has had a series of difficult interviews, he loses sight of the fact that all buyers are human. It is easy to forget that behind the mask which some buyers adopt to ward off too persistent salesmen, there is neither ogre nor saint, but an ordinary person trying to do a job of work to the best of his ability.

In attempting to understand the buyer and his motivations, you must try to understand the man as he really is. There are as many kinds of buyer as there are kinds of human being. In deciding why a buyer adopts a certain attitude to his suppliers, you have to consider not only the particular requirements of his firm, but also his own situation within that firm. The buyer in a large organization is subject to very different pressures to those of his counterpart, in a small firm. He is, very often, a somewhat smaller cog in the wheel—despite the fact that he may be responsible for a much larger purchasing budget. The buyer in a large firm tends to be much more 'corporation-minded'. Company politics play a larger part in shaping his outlook. In certain circumstances he may not have quite the same degree of status as the buyer of a smaller firm. His personal position may be more vulnerable because there are more people willing and able to fill his shoes than would be the case in smaller businesses. It is perhaps for these reasons, coupled with an awareness of his considerable purchasing power, that the large-organization buyer sometimes appears more aggressive, compared with buyers in smaller companies, in his attitude to his suppliers.

Another example of an aggressive buyer is the man who heads a small business which has been built up largely as the result of his own personal effort. Indeed, the main reason for his commercial success may well be his naturally aggressive character. Because he remains acutely conscious of the fact that his business is relatively small, he will instinctively adopt the brisk approach. He will demand immediate action be taken in dealing with all his requests for quotations, samples and deliveries and he will complain violently at any shortcomings in service. He will be quick to take offence at the slightest sign that he and his firm may not be getting priority treatment. Such individuals are understandably jealous of their company's image. They see their firm as an extension of themselves and may react sharply at what they believe to be a reflection upon their company. This can be especially true in connection with account matters. Because they run small businesses, they sometimes have a prejudice against the large organization. They may prefer to deal with suppliers whose businesses are of a similar size to their own. When they have to deal with large firms, they resent any too frequent or too forceful a reminder of their supplier's size and influence.

Use and Abuse of the Notebook

There are divided views among salesmen regarding note-taking during an interview. Some produce their notebook at the outset and proceed to scribble in it throughout the conversation. As a result, they do not need to trust to a capricious memory when they come to write up their sales reports. The method has something to recommend it on the grounds of efficiency; it could also be justified on the grounds that such a display of meticulousness must impress the customer and enhance his confidence in the salesman's business-like approach.

I am all for giving the customer a good impression, but I believe that injudicious use of the notebook can inhibit the conversation. Many people are instinctively put on their guard by the sight of the pencil poised to record their every indiscretion. What might have been a friendly discussion can degenerate into an inquisition.

There is a use for the notebook during interviews, providing it is subtle and unobtrusive. It should only be produced from your pocket or your briefcase to record your customer's specific instructions, such as orders to be placed, samples to be supplied and deliveries to be expedited. (You can of course seize the opportunity thus afforded to scribble a quick note about, say, a competitor's price which was mentioned five minutes previously.) You will soon discover, however that the odd confidence is seldom dropped into the salesman's ear until his notebook has been stowed safely back in his briefcase.

The main need for a notebook comes after the interview is over. All the salient points of the discussion should be recorded immediately, while they are fresh in your mind. Whenever possible this should be done before proceeding to your next call, otherwise you may have difficulty later on in remembering all that has been decided. The notebook also provides a source of reference, in date order, of all your calls over a given period; no doubt you will find it useful to consult your notes just before any subsequent visit.

How to Leave the Door Open for Your Next Visit

Selling to industrial users is a continuing process. A single call seldom produces an order and you will probably have to make a series of visits before you are able to establish regular business. It is therefore important to ensure that, at each call you make on a prospective customer, you provide yourself with a legitimate reason for a subsequent visit.

There are several ways in which this can be done and they all depend on arranging for some agreed action to be taken by your sales office which will need a follow-up call later.

All initial visits made to prospective customers should, ideally, be acknowledged in writing by your sales office. This can be merely a letter thanking the customer for granting you the interview and enclosing sales and technical literature. On receiving such a letter a few days after your visit, the customer will be reminded of your call. He will have a permanent record of your name and your company's name in his files. (Visiting cards have a way of getting lost in desk drawers.) The letter also provides the customer with the name of a contact within your office—a sales clerk or the sales manager—with whom he can communicate should he require additional information or wish to place an order at any time between your visits.

An extension of this is a letter which includes a price list or a quotation based on the customer's specific requirements. Better still, from the point of view of having an excuse for further calls, is the submission of a sample of your product for evaluation.

Each of these actions provides you with a reason for a follow-up visit. You can call, for example, to see if the buyer has read your literature and requires any additional information, to find out if the quotation has been of interest and to check whether the sample has been tested and with what result.

The fact that your company has taken the trouble to send him something which may interest him, places the customer under a certain degree of obligation to see you when you call again. The more legitimate excuses you can find for calling again and again on prospective customers, the greater will be your chances of establishing the kind of relationship needed to get your products considered for purchase.

One has to be careful about this question of persistent calling. A prospective customer will see a salesman frequently if he feels that some purpose is served by doing so. Too frequent calling, will, if it has no apparent purpose other than to badger the buyer provoke resistance. Hence the value of a legitimate reason to 'call back next week'.

CHAPTER EIGHT

ASSESSING THE VALUE OF INFORMATION RECEIVED

Before you start to write your sales report on your visit to the customer, it is advisable to stop for a moment and consider the value of the information you have received. The way in which you write your report will be conditioned by the manner in which you want your sales management to assess the information it contains. We shall deal with the methods of writing reports in a later chapter. At this stage, however, it is necessary that you should apply the information at hand to a critical appraisal, in order to assess its real usefulness to you and to your company.

All that Glisters ...

To pass to your management, by means of your sales reports, incorrect information received from customers can damage your own interests. It will either mislead those responsible for shaping your company's policy or, if they spot the incongruity, make them feel that your assessment is unsound and cause them to place less reliance on your reports in future.

You must therefore judge for yourself the credibility of the information you have been given. At the time of the interview itself, any doubtful statements should be checked by further questioning to ensure that you have not misunderstood what has been said. Even when the information you bring away is, to the best of your belief, that which the customer intended you to receive, you must still question in your own mind the likelihood of its being accurate.

Gullibility is usually the result of a lack of knowledge or the lack of an inquiring mind. You may be forgiven if, in your early days, you fail to reject a piece of information owing to gaps in your knowledge and understanding of the particular industry in which you are engaged. The lack of an inquiring mind, however, is a serious flaw in a sales representative. You must train yourself to be on the look-out for possible deception when getting information about your prospective customers. This is not to be taken as a criticism of the ethics of industrial buyers, for the buyer may have several perfectly valid reasons for not wishing to provide a straight answer to a salesman's question. The buyer's first duty is to safeguard the interests of his firm. Those interests must, on occasion, clash with the salesman's attempts to acquire information about his business. Indeed, the more the salesman persists in trying to obtain information which the buyer is reluctant to provide, the more likely he is to be told something that is inaccurate or misleading.

The type of misleading information which most frequently gets reported by the inexperienced salesman refers to estimates of the customer's quantity requirements. All too often such reports bring a wry smile to the face of the sales manager, who, from his knowledge of the industry, perceives that the figures quoted are grossly exaggerated. The salesman who asks for a sample and a keen quotation on the strength of a buyer's apparent promise of a £100,000 order should examine the facts of the case very carefully to ensure that there is some likelihood of its fulfilment. He may discover that an order of such magnitude will cover all his customer's requirements for ten years. Equally, one would treat with suspicion the information received from a customer who claimed that he could buy a product at 15 per cent off the going price in the trade, especially if one has a number of other customers using similar quantities of the same product who appear happy to continue to reorder without demanding a price reduction.

Why Client Information can be Misleading

Why should your customers give you incorrect information? One reason is that some people, especially those engaged in small-scale businesses, have a natural tendency towards exaggeration. They believe that by 'talking big' they will impress the salesman and therefore obtain priority service or keener prices. This type of customer will give inflated estimates of his requirements, not with any intention to mislead, but to create the impression that he is a big buyer and therefore to be reckoned with.

A far more hazardous situation is where a buyer lets you form the impression that he will order large quantities of goods from you in the hope of extracting a lower price than his true requirements will justify. The irresponsible reporting of such information, without any cautionary qualification on your part, could seriously mislead your management. You may be instructed to bid for this falsely attractive business at a lower price than will be justified by the quantities which actually will be ordered. When the true facts of the case are realized you may find yourself faced with the task of telling the customer that you have made a mistake and that your company cannot confirm the price you have quoted. Such a situation will not enhance your standing with either the customer or your company.

Another trap into which it is easy to fall is to mistake a customer's *potential* usage of a product for his *current* usage. The customer may state that he will require x thousand tons. In fact his current usage may be half that quantity, but he has the expectation of a large contract which, if obtained, will double his requirements. He may not think it necessary to explain to the salesman that the figure he has quoted is conditional upon his getting this contract.

The salesmen should *always* look a gift horse in the mouth. When an order comes your way unexpectedly, you should ask yourself how and why you got it. To imagine that you have won the business because you are a first-class salesman may be a delusion. The motivations which have caused the customer to select your company as his supplier should be studied as an object lesson for the future.

There are many reasons why customers change their suppliers, but there is one which it could be dangerous to overlook. If a firm is buying goods on credit and falls behind in settling its account, the supplier in question will ultimately have to 'put the bar up' to further deliveries until the account situation is rectified. When this occurs, the customer must either pay his bills or seek further supplies on credit elsewhere. If he turns to you and gives you a large order for no apparent reason, you would be well advised to think carefully—and to caution your management to think carefully—before making many deliveries on credit. The previous supplier may decide to cut his loss and, by taking legal action to recover the debt, force the customer into liquidation: the chances of your deliveries being paid for in full would then be very slender indeed.

How to Cross-examine the Information You Receive

How, then, should you go about the task of cross-examining the information you have been given by the customer? The answer lies in balancing the likelihood of its accuracy against your knowledge of the market in general and what you already know about this customer in particular.

Attention has already been drawn to the need to understand the motivations of individual buyers. In the present context one must consider the probability that he would mislead you, either intentionally or unintentionally. The man who is precise and meticulous in the way he conducts his business is unlikely to exaggerate, unwittingly, the quantities of a product he expects to use over a given period. The buyer who is well known and highly respected in the industry as a reasonable individual is unlikely to inflate his requirements to trick you into quoting your bulk-quantity price for what will later turn out to be only a moderate order. On the other hand, if you suddenly get an unexpected order from a firm which has expanded very fast and is known to be short of working capital, you should ask yourself whether your luck is as good as it seems. If you know that the current supplier provides a good product, with a reliable delivery service and at a keen price, you may wonder if it is safe to accept the order without some safeguard that payment will be received promptly when due.

It is a question not only of judgment based on knowledge and experience, neither of which will you have in abundance in the early days of your career, but also of awareness. Once you are aware of the hazards which may exist, you can be on the look-out for them. Where there is a doubt in your mind about the veracity of your information, or the desirability of taking business at a particular account, you should bring the matter to the attention of your sales management. Even if your doubts prove unjustified, you will have acted in a responsible manner and the only reflection upon you will be one of credit.

Deciding the Further Action Required to Obtain Business

Once you have confirmed the accuracy of your information, you have to put it to use. Your initial call on a new account will have been mainly a fact-finding mission. The task of selling must now begin in earnest.

The factors to be considered in achieving business may be summarized as follows:

(a) The customer's propensity to buy.
(b) The availability of the product he needs.
(c) The competitive merit of your company.
(d) The desire of your company for the business.
(e) The relative value of the business.

(a) The Customer's Propensity to Buy

In an earlier chapter I posed the question: Why should the customer buy your product? Now we have to ask ourselves. Does he want to buy? The answer is important. If it is in the affirmative, the chances of establishing business, while by no means a foregone conclusion, are at least promising. If the answer is negative, one's calculations must be based on an extended time-scale before success can be expected.

(b) The Availability of the Product

One must decide not only whether the type of product, but also whether the grade of that product which the customer needs for his particular application, can be supplied. The need to marry the product to the application has already been emphasized. If the customer's requirements in this respect are critical, considerable technical work may be involved before a suitable quality can be produced to satisfy the specific needs of the application.

(c) The Competitive Merit of Your Company

If the merits of your company are such as to have a particular appeal to this customer, your chances of obtaining business will be good. However, if any of your company's policies seem to be in opposition to the particular needs of this customer, you will have to consider them and do something about them. A simple example is afforded by the question of discounts and credit facilities.

Suppose your company, as a matter of policy, does not offer cash discounts and refuses to give more than, say, 60 days' credit. If one of your customers insists on a discount, or on a minimum of 90 days' credit, you will have to ask your management to modify its policy if it wants you to get this particular piece of business.

(d) The Desire of Your Company for the Business

Upon the desirability of the business to your management will depend the extent of any special assistance they will provide to enable you to get it. If a lot of technical work is involved in the development of a special grade, if plant has to be adapted to make the product, if special stock-holding arrangements are required, you will need the management's full interest and support for the project. If there is little desire on the part of your management for this particular business, you may find your efforts to sell to this account frustrated.

(e) The Relative Value of this Business

There is no point in devoting a high proportion of your precious calling time to the pursuit of a piece of business which is of only moderate value to your company. If you do, you are probably going to have to neglect more important opportunities elsewhere. Equally, if you think that your prospects of securing this piece of business are only moderate, you should concentrate your efforts on those other customers where, by comparison, successful results seem more assured.

Your decision to compete for a particular piece of business, or not to compete, rests on a consideration of all the above factors.

Clearly, if the customer shows little inclination to buy from your company, you will have to take a long term view of your prospects. You may decide that, given time and with regular calling, you will be able to reverse his attitude. If you do not have exactly the product he needs, you will have to find out whether your management would be prepared to manufacture it. This would require special development work, which may be costly and of long duration. Your company will have to weigh the value of the business against that of other projects to which its development resources may already be allocated. Much will depend on the strength of the case you make to your management. Finally, you will have to ask yourself how much of your selling efforts should be devoted to this particular account. If your efforts are dispersed too widely you may fail to bring any one of your projects to fruition.

Having made your decision to go for the business, the next step is to consider the requirements which the customer has laid down as the conditions under which he will buy from you. These will vary from account to account, but will usually include the following:

(*a*) Grade or quality of the product.
(*b*) Price.
(*c*) The degree of service, including delivery arrangements, special stock-holding and packing.
(*d*) The amount of credit and length of credit.

These are the specific points which you should itemize in your sales report to your management as the conditions under which business at this account may be obtained. If you have to obtain special instructions or special action from your management in order to meet any of these conditions, you should try to provide in your report as much supporting information as you can.

(*a*) Grade or Quality of the Product

If the application for which your product is to be used requires a special quality or non-standard grade, you should furnish your management with details of the processing conditions under which the customer will operate and the performance he expects of the product in service. Should you be attempting to take business away from a competitor, then that supplier's name and the grade he is supplying should be reported.

(*b*) Price

If it is necessary to depart from your standard price, or if you do not have a standard price (as with a special grade, for example), you will have to obtain authorization from your management to quote specially. In order to reach a decision they will need to know the price at which the customer is likely to place the business and, if you are proposing to take the business away from a competitor, what is the competitor's price.

(*c*) The Degree of Service

If the customer's requirements are such that your normal delivery and packing arrangements are inadequate, you will have to tell the management exactly what special facilities will be needed.

(*d*) The Amount of Credit and Length of Credit

Companies vary in their policies with regard to account matters. In many cases the salesman is expected to discuss with a new customer the payment arrangements which are to be agreed. Before an account is opened, it is usual to seek references from the customer's bank and from two or more firms who have had trading experience with him. When a customer asks for extended credit, i.e. the facility of settling his accounts within an extended period of time, your accounts manager is likely to ask for more than the usual amount of information regarding the customer's financial standing. He may wish to see a balance sheet and, particularly in the case of a small firm, may require some form of personal guarantee from the proprietor or, in the case of a limited company, from the directors.

When a customer requests special credit facilities, you are entitled to inquire whether he is prepared to disclose his financial position to your company. A customer who asks for extended credit is, in fact, asking your firm to lend him money. No one, be he a bank manager, a manager of a finance house, or a private individual, lends money without first assuring himself that the borrower is a 'fair risk'.

Upon receipt of your report setting out the above requirements, your sales management will be in a position to decide whether or not they are able, and willing, to satisfy the customer's demands. Their willingness to undertake special development work, to sanction a special price, to agree special credit facilities, will depend in considerable measure upon the strength of the case which you have presented in your sales report.

CHAPTER NINE

SALES REPORTS AND HOW TO WRITE THEM

Every firm has its own means by which adequate communication is maintained between the sales representative and his sales office; the choice of method is the responsibility of the management. It is, however, very much in the salesman's interests that such communication should be really adequate and a vital part of his work is to ensure that it is maintained.

In small firms, employing one or perhaps two representatives, verbal contact by telephone or by personal visits to the sales office may suffice. In larger companies, however, and where the products to be sold are of a sophisticated nature, it is generally accepted that the representative should write a sales report for every visit he makes to a customer.

For some people the writing of reports can be a difficult and tedious chore, the least pleasing aspect of their work. The ability to write lucid reports is, nevertheless, of considerable importance to the progress of your career and one you would be well advised to acquire as quickly as possible.

The effectiveness of a salesman, particularly one whose territory is distant from his head office and who is seldom seen in person by his superiors, is judged largely by the way in which he presents himself in his reports. No salesman, one hopes, would wish to appear seedily dressed and unshaven before his sales manager or his directors. He would hardly expect to create a good impression. Equally, he should not present himself in writing in a manner which is off-hand, careless and untidy. His sales reports should always be as carefully considered and as well groomed as his personal appearance.

Why Sales Reports are Necessary

At the end of a busy day, considerable stamina is demanded of the salesman who must sit down and commit to paper a résumé of each call he has made; which is why the task is too often performed in a perfunctory manner. By understanding the value of your reports it is to be hoped that you will reject the slipshod approach, set yourself a high standard of reporting and provide a creditable impression of your dedication to your work.

Sales reports are necessary for the following four main reasons:

(a) Information Regarding the Salesman

Reports keep the sales management informed as to the activities of the representative. They indicate the number of customers and potential customers he has visited, the frequency of his visits and the degree of efficiency with which he is utilizing his time. The management are therefore in a position to judge the salesman's overall effectiveness and whether the area is being covered adequately.

(b) Market Intelligence

Reports provide an information service on the conditions prevailing in the market. They are an indicator of expansion, stagnation or recession within the industry. In order to formulate suitable policies, the management must be kept informed of the general reception of the company's products in the field and whether the present quality, service and prices are adequate to meet the requirements of the market.

(c) Customer Case-histories

The report also provides a permanent case-history for each account. If it is ever necessary at any time to ascertain the background to past negotiations, the customer's requirements, his ordering pattern or his credit-worthiness, the report is an obvious source of reference.

(d) Communication Between Salesman and Sales Office

It is by means of his sales report that the salesman makes known to his management the detail of the current situation at specific accounts, the prospects of future business and his recommendations for action to be taken by the sales office.

It will be seen that the sales report is a vital document, both to the sales representative and to his management. It is the essential link between the two, enabling the salesman to inform, advise, comment upon and, if the need arises, to criticize the situation which exists between the company and the customer.

How Sales Reports are Used

How sales reports are used depends on the system in operation in the sales department and on the degree of importance attached to them by the management personnel. In large industrial companies, copies of sales reports may be circulated and scrutinized by several members of the management staff. Each executive will use them in a slightly different way. Some of these uses are as follows:

(a) By the Marketing Manager

The marketing manager's aim is to establish trading policies which achieve the most profitable utilization of his company's resources. He will therefore use the sales report as a means of observing market trends, of following the progress of his own policies and of monitoring the policies of his competitors. For him the most significant items in the report will be those which refer to changes in customer demand, either in volume or in quality, movements in price and the activities of competitors.

(b) By the Sales Manager

It is the function of the sales manager to promote and maintain sales turnover at a level, and within a price policy, laid down by the marketing department. Sales reports provide him with information on the activities of his representatives in the field and on what progress, if any, is being made with individual accounts. They enable him to advise and direct the salesman in his approach to his work. They inform him of the value of potential business, of the security of existing business, of complaints relating to quality and service and of any special action required to maintain and extend his sales.

(c) By the Accounts Manager

The accounts manager of an industrial company is responsible, among other duties, for the provision of suitable credit facilities to customers and for ensuring that payments are received when due. For him, the content of a sales report is a barometer of the financial viability of the customer. He will be particularly interested in those items which refer to the customer's trading situation: whether he is finding business good, above average or below average. He will want to know of any proposed expansion of the customer's premises, the purchase of new equipment and plans to alter the scope of his operations. Any such changes to the existing situation could, under certain circumstances, affect the customer's financial position.

(d) By the Sales-Office Clerical Personnel

The clerical personnel in the sales office handle routine actions requested by the representative in his reports, subject to any special instructions given to them by the sales manager. Correspondence clerks are responsible for writing letters, preparing quotations and handling telephonic communication with the customer. The order clerk will arrange for samples and for the progressing of orders at the request of the representative.

Thus the sales report is many things to many people within the organization. This plurality of use should be borne in mind when the report is written. In some firms the individual functions of management referred to above may be combined. The sales manager may, for instance, be responsible for both marketing and sales. He may also be responsible for the amount of credit to be given to individual accounts. In a small business the proprietor or one of the directors may be responsible for the whole selling operation. However large or small your management may be, the use to which your reports will be put will be equally varied. In the final analysis, the use which is made of a sales report will depend on the information it contains and the manner in which it is presented.

In a firm which employs a large number of sales representatives, the reading of sales reports represents a considerable task for the management personnel. The executives concerned must read every report to ensure that they are up to date with the current situation in the market and with each individual customer. To skim too rapidly through a pile of reports is to run the risk of missing information which may be vital. An alert manager cannot afford to delegate the reading of sales reports to a subordinate. In certain circumstances—and these are the ones that are likely to matter most—he alone will be in a position to judge the significance of the information provided. Items which his subordinate might pass over as irrelevant may prove to be of prime importance, especially if taken in conjunction with information drawn from other sources.

The typical salesman is not, unfortunately, a good writer of English. Too many sales reports are written hastily, at the end of the day when the salesman is tired and impatient to finish his work. As a result, he is content to scribble a hasty jumble of facts without form or clarity. The unfortunate reader is forced to pick his way slowly and with caution if he is to make any sense of the information provided.

The salesman who writes in this fashion does himself a disservice. In the first place he irritates the reader, who asks why the writer cannot say simply what he means. Secondly, he runs the risk that his words may be misconstrued, and the information and opinions he is trying to convey may be dismissed by his management as inaccurate or irrelevant.

How Reports Should Be Written

If you intend to perform any task to the best of your ability, you must approach it in the right frame of mind. Nobody can hope to write a good report when he is mentally tired, short of time, or anxious to 'dash the thing off' before going to play tennis or watch television.

The human mind tends to function at its best when following the well trodden path of habit. The wise salesman, therefore, sets aside a specific time of day to write his reports. He allows himself perhaps an hour or an hour and a half each evening for this purpose. The time to sit down and write is not immediately after you have parked your car after a lengthy journey. The mind as well as the body needs refreshment and relaxation. Many salesmen prefer to allow themselves an hour or so in which to have a meal and 'unwind' before they settle down to write their reports.

Some novice sales representatives view with dismay the thought of having to work every evening. They regard this as their free time and envy their neighbours who are out mowing their lawns or on their way to the pub or the cinema. It is an understandable attitude, but one must take a broader view. Since sales representation may be regarded as a profession, one cannot expect to work a nine-to-five stint and then finish for the day. The salesman is, of course, entitled to his leisure and, providing he organizes himself properly, he can have and enjoy it. The work he does, however, is not dull routine. Every day offers the challenge of visiting different places and meeting different people. It is very largely an open-air job and not subject to quite the same pressures as office- or factory-bound occupations.

To write lucidly, one must first marshal one's facts. It helps if you have a logical mind. If you have not, efforts must be made to adopt a logical approach to the information you wish to impart. The matter to be reported should be subdivided and set out under sub-headings. Sentences should be as short as possible. The long, unwieldy sentence demands far greater concentration on the part of the reader than a short one. Paragraphs, too, should be kept short and consist of no more than two or three sentences.

Do not assume that your reader is immediately familiar with the detail of the situation. Ensure that each report contains a brief reference to the existing situation before the new information is provided. It will assist your management personnel to 'pick up the threads' quickly, especially when they have to read 20 or more reports in one sitting. Differentiate clearly between what has been stated to you by the customer as facts and what is only your own interpretation of the facts.

If a customer has given you information which he has asked you to treat as confidential, state this in your report. Of course, when a customer tells you something 'off the record', he knows that he is speaking to your company through you and that you will report his statements to your management. But a cautionary comment that this piece of information has been given to you in confidence will avoid needless embarrassment to the individual concerned should one of your managers have occasion to speak to another person in the client company.

The first paragraph of your report should state the purpose of the visit. Many salesmen overlook the fact that their calls should have a specific purpose. 'Oh, I was in the area, so I called in', or, 'It was some time since I had been there, so I thought I had better make a call', are the kind of response one often gets when the question is asked: 'Why did you make this visit?' This is a very unprofessional way of carrying on.

Every visit should have a purpose and the report should state that purpose. The management are entitled to know the motivation which caused you to visit the customer.

The second paragraph should deal with the main subject of your visit. Succeeding paragraphs, under suitable sub-headings, should deal with any other items discussed. Opinions and comment on the part of the author should generally be kept to the end and entered under a suitable title such as 'Remarks'.

Finally, the action required to be taken should be shown at the end of the report. This should state what is to be done by management or sales-office personnel and also what is to be done by the representative himself. Each action item should be numbered.

In the examples which follow I have set out to illustrate how the same information gained by a representative might be presented (*a*) incorrectly and (*b*) correctly, according to the way the report is written. No one system of reporting is universal and every company has its own report format devised to suit its particular requirements. For the purposes of these illustrations, however, it has been assumed that no itemized report sheet has been provided by the company concerned and the method of presentation has been left to the discretion of the representative.

Example 1 (a)

Visit of J. Smith to Nuts & Bolts Ltd., Barchester

Called to see Mr. Brown but his secretary said he was away till Saturday. I saw Mr. Jones instead, he is new here. He said he did not think that the sample of the red special grade had been tested. I asked him what our chances were of getting an order for the clear material and he said that it would be up to Mr. Brown and I would have to see him next week. I will try and fix an appointment to do this because their factory is outside Barchester and he is often there instead of his office. Mr. Jones said they were buying a new machine and would be using a lot more material later this year but he thought they could buy a lot cheaper than £0·12½ per lb. I said I would find out if we could offer a better price than £0·12½. He said he would try and run the red sample at the weekend if it had not already been done. He will see Mr. Brown about it when he comes back on Saturday. He gave me an order for 2 tons of standard black that he wants delivered in a week's time. Can we do this?

J. Smith

In the above report, on what is obviously a follow-up visit, the representative provides a reasonable amount of information. None of it is very precise. He was unfortunate in that he did not see Mr. Brown, who would apparently have been better informed and might have been able to make a decision regarding the 'clear material'. However, the call was not wasted: he got an order, he found out about a new machine and he picked up Mr. Jones's comment regarding a price which had been quoted.

We are not concerned here with the effectiveness of the interview so much as with the way in which it has been reported. The first point to note is that, unless one is closely familiar with what has gone on before at this account, references to 'red special grade' or 'the clear material' mean very little. Obviously, every firm has its own internal references to its grades and products which would be meaningless to an outsider. In this instance, however, it is doubtful if his own management will know precisely to what J. Smith is referring when he uses such vague terminology. He has made the mistake of assuming that everyone who reads his report will know the detail as well as he does himself.

Secondly, by jumbling his facts, he has given us a somewhat confused picture of the situation with this customer. To grasp fully what is going on, it will probably be necessary to re-read the report, mentally underlining the salient points.

Let us now set out the same facts in a form that is easier for the reader to assimilate.

Example 1 (b)

Customer: Nuts & Bolts Ltd., Canal Street, Barchester
Date Visited: 30th January 19. .
Person Interviewed: Mr. J. Jones (Assistant Buyer)

The purpose of this visit was to check if the sample of Red 51038/77 (Special) submitted 15th January for their signal-lamp job had been tested. Also to ask for an initial order for Clear 7962/E following their approval of this grade in December.

Red 5/038/77 (Special). In the absence of Mr. Brown (Chief Buyer) I saw Mr. Jones who was unable to give me any definite information. The sample, if not already tested, may be tried this weekend.

Clear 7962/E. No decision has yet been reached regarding the promised order. Mr. Jones suggested that a competitor (unnamed) had quoted below £0·12½ per lb. (I will check with Mr. Brown next week).

Standard Black P125H. New order for 2 tons received for delivery in 7 days. (Order attached to this report.)

New Plant. Mr. Jones said they were buying a new machine. He did not know its size or make. He said their consumption of material would therefore increase later this year.

Further Action. (1) Order Section please note new order for Black P125H.

(2) J. Smith to see Mr. Brown in four weeks' time.

J. Smith

All the facts are there, each subject is itemized and all the grades discussed have been given their code references to avoid any confusion. Everyone in the company, from the managing director to the office boy, can understand what it is all about.

Example 2 (a)

Visit of J. Robinson to Sweet, Tooth & Co., Oxbridge

Mr Tooth said that the lids for their sweet jars have been cracking in the shops and their customers have been complaining. Apparently these lids are made for them by a firm called Ace Moulding in Barchester. Their deliveries have not been very good, either. So it has been decided that they will make them themselves in future. I heard about this in the trade, which is why I called.

Ace have been making these lids for about 10 years using Elephantine material. Mr. Tooth said he did not think much of their material, it was probably the reason for their getting so many breakages.

Sweet, Tooth are putting up a new building on waste ground behind their factory and expect to mould 350,000 lids next year. Last year they bought 200,000 lids from Ace. The lids weigh 3 ozs. each and are in black, white and yellow. They want a sample of AX3 Black by July 8th when their new 16 oz. machine should be ready. There will be 30 tons of black and 10 tons each of yellow and white. All will be taken in 5 ton deliveries.

I quoted him £300 a ton for AX3 and he said that Elephantine's price was 'a shade lower'. It seems that Super Colossal have quoted £300. He is getting samples from both and will run these with our sample in July before he finally decides on his supplier.

Please confirm our price by letter.

J. Robinson

This is a reasonably lucid report into which the writer has condensed a considerable number of facts. There is nothing which is remarkably bad about the style, but once again the method of presentation leaves something to be desired. It would be easier to follow if these facts, which are very important to an understanding of the situation, were presented in a more orderly fashion, using sub-headings.

Example 2 (b)

Customer: Sweet, Tooth & Co. Ltd
Date Visited: 30th January 19..
Person Interviewed: Mr. William Tooth (Director)

Visit made following information received that this firm intended
to start injection moulding their jar lids in polyethylene.

Current Situation

Sweet, Tooth & Co. are old established confectionary manufacturers, specializing in boiled sweets. The bulk of their production is
supplied direct to retailers in glass jars and up to ten years ago metal
closures were used. Since then they have bought in their jar lids from
the Ace Moulding Co. of Barchester who provide a 3 oz. closure in
three colours: black, white and yellow. In recent months, deliveries
from Ace have been protracted. Also, on several occasions Sweet,
Tooth have had to complain of breakage of lids in use.

Future Plans

Because their usage of lids is increasing (200,000 last year; 350,000
expected next year), they have decided to put in plant to make their
own closures. A factory extension of some 50,000 sq. ft. is under way
and a new Master-Mould machine is on order.

They expect to have machine and mould ready by July and to
commence production in August this year.

Annual usage of material will be about 50 tons, with deliveries in
5 ton lots.

Colour breakdown is :   30 tons black
                 10 tons white
                 10 tons yellow

Action Taken During This Visit

I have quoted our list price, for grade AX3, at £300 per ton and
promised a sample in black by 8th July.

Competitor's Activity

Super Colossal are reputed to have quoted £300 per ton. Mr. Tooth
says that the Elephantine Company's price is 'a shade lower'. Both
companies have promised samples for trial.

Conclusions and Recommendations

In spite of Elephantine's alleged lower price, I doubt if Mr. Tooth
will use their material. He told me that Ace Moulding had been using
Elephantine material and he thought this had been partly the cause of

the trouble he had with their lids. Super Colossal's service to this area is not good at the moment. We should, therefore, get this business.

No decision will, however, be made regarding supplier until all samples have been tested in July.

Action to be Taken by the Sales Dept.
(1) Letter to be sent for the attention of Mr. W. Tooth, confirming my visit and quotation for AX3 colours in 5 ton lots at £300 per ton.
(2) Submit sample of Black AX3 by 8th July latest.

J. Robinson

Example 3 (a)

Visit of J. Brown to the Black & White Furniture Manufacturing Co.
Interviewed: Mr. White (Works Director).
Date of Visit: 15th September 19. .

Mr. White said he was very annoyed because we were late delivering his last order for Olive Green Q693, and the 200 gallons of White Q767 supplied against our delivery note No. 19427 on 12th July was off-shade. He said he could not understand what had happened to our service and quality lately. He had always been able to rely on us but just recently we were making so many mistakes and forgetting to deal with things that he was not sure whether he wanted to go on dealing with us. It was a very difficult interview and what made matters worse was that he asked our office to send him a colour chart of matt-finish lacquers as long ago as the 19th of August and nothing has been done about it. I have known Fred White for a long time and he has always been a good friend to us but if we go on like this we shall lose all his business.

He wanted the colour chart because they are thinking of making a new range of nursery furniture and he had the buyer from one of his biggest customers coming in to see him about it. When ours did not turn up he had to show him Glorious Varnish's colour range and he chose five of their standard colours. This has lost us at least 300 gallons of business.

I asked him what he wanted us to do about the off-shade White Q767 and he said he could use up 75 gallons on internal parts but he wants the rest replaced as quickly as possible. So far as the Olive Green is concerned, he wants this for kitchen-cabinet fronts for Afghanistan. Their agent got this order in spite of strong competition, and he had to dispatch the cabinets by 30th August at the latest to catch the boat sailing on 1st September. Our paint arrived too late and now he expects that the order will be cancelled.

J. Brown

No doubt, upon reading this report, the sales manager will be alarmed by the apparent failure of the company to provide satisfactory quality and service. He will want to take immediate action to correct the faults and reassure the customer in order to retain his future business. The first difficulty he will face, however, is to understand exactly what has happened and what action his own man-on-the-spot recommends. Before he can do anything about the problems which have been reported to him, he has to read the report again to sort out the mixture of facts and opinion. How very much more effective this report would be if presented in a more concise form.

Example 3 (b)

Customer: Black & White Furniture Manufacturing Co.
Interviewed: Mr. White (Works Director)
Date of Visit: 15th September 19..

This customer expressed extreme annoyance caused by failures in our quality and service during recent weeks and threatened not to place further business with us.

Olive Green Q693

We were due to deliver 150 gallons against their order No. 92 on 25th August. Delivery was actually made on 30th August (five days late). See our delivery note No. 19635. They had a consignment of kitchen cabinets for Afghanistan which were due for dispatch to catch a boat sailing 1st September. The late arrival of our paint prevented them from meeting their commitments and Mr. White expects to have his order cancelled. The business in Afghanistan is important to him and was obtained by his agent in spite of strong competition.

White Q767

We supplied 200 gallons of Standard White Q767 (our delivery note No. 19427) on 12th July which is off-shade. This colour is used for drawer fronts and I can confirm that the last consignment does not match the colour of previous deliveries. Mr. White can use 75 gallons on internal parts but wants the remainder replaced as quickly as possible.

Colour Charts of Matt-Finish Lacquers

Mr. White said that he telephoned our office on 19th August and asked for a colour chart of matt-finish lacquers. It appears that he may be producing a range of nursery furniture and wished to show our colours to the buyer of his largest customer. He did not receive our chart and consequently had to show the colour range of Glorious

Varnish, with the result that five of their colours have been selected. This lost opportunity may have cost us 300 gallons of future business at this account.

Comment and Recommendations

Mr. White said that he could not understand what had happened to our service and quality lately. He had always been able to rely on us in the past, but if these recent failures were to continue he could not be sure that he would want to go on dealing with us.

I have known Fred White for a long time and he has always been a good friend to us. I believe he means what he says and we may lose this business.

I suggest the following immediate action be taken:

(1) Deliver 125 gallons White Q767 in correct colour and collect an equal quantity of off-shade paint delivered on 12th July.

(2) Investigate cause of White Q767 supplied against delivery note No. 19427 being off-shade.

(3) Investigate cause of delay in delivery of Olive Green Q693 against their order No. 92.

(4) Investigate failure on the part of the Sales Office to send the colour chart of matt-finish lacquers requested by Mr. White on 19th August.

(5) A letter of apology to be sent addressed for the attention of Mr. F. White.

(6) J. Brown to call again after delivery of replacement White Q767 to ensure that it is satisfactory.

J. Brown

CHAPTER TEN

HOW TO SECURE AN ORDER

There are times when securing an order is almost as tantalizing as trying to net a butterfly: however carefully one plans one's approach, at the very moment when success seems certain it flutters off just far enough to be out of reach.

We have already established that the salesman must sell himself to his customer. Too often, however, a salesman can become so absorbed in the projection of his own personality that he forgets the essential purpose of his visit. He establishes an excellent personal relationship with the buyer and is then reluctant to press for the order, as though it were bad form to do so.

It is not always easy to make the customer understand that, however enjoyable the afternoon round of golf or the after-dinner cigars, it is the order that matters ultimately. Some sales representatives are hampered by a feeling that it is impolite to press too hard for business, as though one were raising a controversial issue at the vicarage tea-party. This is one of the dangers which result from a lack of professionalism: it is a by-product of too great a degree of personal friendship between seller and buyer.

Why Your First Call may not Produce an Order

Industrial companies seldom make a decision to place business until they know something of the kind of firm with whom they are dealing. The customer needs to assure himself, not only that the quality of the product he buys will be satisfactory, but also that the potential supplier can provide the service he needs. Most industrial selling is not a question of getting a single order (except, possibly, in the field of capital equipment) but of ensuring repeat business. The supplier/customer relationship is, therefore, likely to be continuous over months and years to come. To insist upon an order at the time of your first call would be unrealistic. The customer has to be given time to get used to the idea of placing his business with you. Before he enters into any commitments, he may wish to make a few inquiries about you, your firm and your products. Before he changes his source of supply he may decide to consult the opinion of others within his firm, including his technical and production colleagues. It is also likely that he will want to evaluate samples of your product before any decision is made.

Should the quality or the price of the product you are offering appear more attractive than the quality or price he enjoys from his current supplier, his first thought will be to tackle that supplier to see if he will meet your competition. There is nothing remarkable in this. If you and your company were holding the business and your customer received a better offer from one of your competitors, you would expect to be given the opportunity to match that offer before the business was taken from you.

Because all these activities on the part of the prospective customer take time, it is unrealistic to expect a decision to be reached at the first call. Whether greater progress can be made on the second visit will depend upon its timing and upon the degree of urgency with which the buyer has set about his inquiries.

The Need for Persistence

The only way in which you will ultimately secure orders is by persistence. Buyers are busy men, with many calls on their time. When it is important to a buyer to find an alternative source of supplies he will often reach a quick decision. Where his normal supply source is generally acceptable, however, he is unlikely to consider that a decision to make a change is of overriding importance. Indeed, he may have other pressures on his time, other negotiations in hand, which are of far greater importance to him than the one in which you are concerned. In the fullness of time he will get around to dealing with your particular offer, but this could be weeks or even months away. You must therefore keep up the pressure by reminding the buyer that he has to make this particular decision.

You should not, of course, be unreasonable in the demands you place on the buyer. He must be given adequate time to complete his necessary preparations. Just how long a time is to be considered adequate will depend on the relative importance of the items in the buyer's purchasing arrangements. If it is comparatively small from the buyer's point of view, he may be able to reach a decision without a great deal of preparation. However, just because it is of limited importance to him, he may give it a low priority and the decision may have to wait its turn.

Where the piece of business under discussion represents a major purchasing item, there can be other reasons for delay. Although he himself may be prepared to give it high priority, just because it is an important matter the buyer will have to consult his colleagues. He will also have to speak to his current supplier and give him a reasonable time in which to decide whether he wishes to meet your competition.

Your degree of persistence will, therefore, have to be conditional according to the circumstances. If you press too hard for a decision before the buyer has had time to consider all the issues, you will run the risk of spoiling your advantageous position. Business opportunities can be lost by the over-zealous salesman who, by chasing the customer for a decision too soon, merely causes annoyance and irritation. The buyer may begin to have second thoughts about the desirability of placing his business in the hands of a company whose representative is over-persistent. He may even begin to wonder if your firm is short of work and this can lead him to wonder about the true competitiveness of your quality and service.

The Need to Force a Decision

There are times when it becomes necessary to force the customer to make the decision to buy. This situation is not reached until he has had adequate time to complete his preparatory work. When this has been done, however, you are entitled to know his decision. Just as there are salesmen who find it difficult to press for an order, so there are buyers who are reluctant to tell the salesman he is not going to get one. All buyers are human and there are many good-natured people who, as buyers, are embarrassed by the thought of hurting the salesman's feelings. Such a buyer will postpone telling you that he has decided not to change his source of supply, especially when you and your company have gone to a lot of trouble to try and get the business. When a salesman has provided everything for which he has been asked, the buyer feels obliged to give him some business. Very often the reason for the buyer's reluctance to change is simply that he feels an equal obligation to his existing supplier.

This situation occurs frequently in business dealings and one can sympathize with the buyer's predicament. We have talked of tough, aggressive buyers motivated by prejudice. There are many others who are just ordinary, rational individuals who wish to be fair to both their current and their potential suppliers.

A buyer faced with these conflicting pressures often avoids making a decision simply by allowing the business to remain with his current supplier; meanwhile he puts off the potential supplier with vague excuses and half-promises for the future. When this situation is reached, the buyer may need to be pressurized for his own good. It is a question of knowing the right time to strike the final blow. One may usefully bear in mind the simile of the good general who, having seen the battle reach a critical stage, knows when he must commit his final reserves to achieve a decision. If you commit your final reserves of pressure on the buyer either too soon or too late, the business may be lost. The good salesman soon acquires the 'feel' of negotiations and knows instinctively when it is time to strike to get his order.

Means of Forcing a Sale

(a) The Customer's Need for an Alternative Supplier

In industrial selling it is not always necessary to remove the current supplier to obtain business for one's company. Many firms find it desirable to have at least two suppliers. Continuity of supply is essential to the mass-production process. A factory which is set up to produce, let us say, a packaging container for a food product, must maintain its output in spite of breakdowns in its supplier's plant caused by faulty equipment, labour disputes, fire, flood or the like. Such interruption in the supply of materials and components is a constant hazard. It can occur even when every precaution has been taken on the part of the supplier company. It is, therefore, an essential insurance for the large user of a product to have an alternative source of supply.

This need for an alternative supply source can provide an important opportunity for the industrial salesman. Some customers may contend that, while they actually buy from one source only, they are in touch with other suppliers from whom they could, if necessary, draw in supplies. This may be true where smallish quantities of a product are involved, but a large-volume user would be foolish to imagine that he could obtain supplies of a specialized product at very short notice from a firm with whom he was not currently doing business. No doubt the potential supplier would do all he could to take advantage of the opportunity suddenly presented to him. But it would be an exceptional supplier who could place at the customer's disposal a large proportion of his capacity within a matter of days. By the time he had so arranged his production to make bulk supplies of the product available, the existing supplier would probably have got over his difficulties. Meanwhile, however, the customer's production line would have stopped, with possibly disastrous results. This is why the responsible buyer prefers to have at least two *active* sources of supply.

There are two further advantages to the customer in having more than one supplier. The first is economic: the buyer, should he consider it necessary, can play off one supplier against another on price. The other is technical. The firm which offers a slight technical superiority over its rival can rightly claim a larger share of the available business; the other supplier will be compelled, if he wishes to establish an equal share, to match this technical proficiency.

This question of dual sources of supply presents not only opportunities but also possible hazards. If the customer has, currently, only one active source of supply, the salesman can press him to split his business and give him at least a part share. Very often, it is not necessary to take business off another supplier. Where a customer's requirements are increasing rapidly, the existing business may be left with the original supplier and a new supplier brought in to take up the increase.

However, where two suppliers are already entrenched at an account, the prospective supplier may find himself in some difficulty. The customer may be reluctant to consider a third source for fear that, by subdividing his business so much, the quantity he has to place with each party will be relatively unimportant to them and he will no longer get their best attention. On the other hand, the customer who already has two suppliers may find that one of them is not satisfactory and may be prepared to replace him. In so doing he will risk disruption to only a part of his supplies, and this may make him more inclined to take a chance.

(b) The Need for a Bulk Trial

Mention has already been made of the submission of samples and of price negotiations. Even when the customer's requirements appear to have been met on the question of quality and price, he may still be reluctant to make the final decision. It demands courage on the part of a customer to change suppliers, especially where business has been placed with one source for a long period of time. If the first bulk deliveries from the new supplier vary from his sample, whoever has made the purchasing decision will lay himself open to a charge of costing his firm a lot of money in wasted production time. Anything which the prospective supplier can do to alleviate this problem can only assist his cause.

One such means is a willingness to supply a bulk quantity of his product for trial. Sometimes this is offered on a sale-or-return basis with an understanding that, if the customer is dissatisfied with the performance of the product, the supplier will collect it without argument.

When a salesman is able to get his customer and his management to agree to such an arrangement, he exposes his delivery service, his packing and handling processes as well as his production quality, to the inspection of the customer's production management. He has progressed beyond the commercial buyer and got his product, in bulk, on to the shop floor. Furthermore, he may be able to arrange for members of his own technical department to be present when the trial quantity is processed under actual production conditions.

If his product is all that he has claimed it to be, this bulk quantity should process at least as well as that of the competitor which is currently being used. It may well exhibit certain processing advantages, and thus recommend itself to the customer's production personnel. Far from opposing any change in their source of supply, they may well encourage the buyer to consider your company as a regular supplier for the future.

With large-volume users, the salesman should as a matter of course aim for a bulk trial of his product whenever the opportunity to arrange one presents itself.

(c) The Price Question

A situation to be avoided in pressing for business arises where a buyer suggests to the potential supplier that a price, lower than he is currently paying, will secure him the business. The price is then passed to the current supplier who, rather than lose the business, feels obliged to meet it even though it means cutting his profit margin.

An exercise of this kind does not get the salesman any nearer to acquiring the business. Indeed, it only makes his future situation more difficult: having forced his competitor's price down, he has to meet a lower price when he next makes a bid for the business.

If you have reason to believe that you are faced with a customer who might 'use' your quotation in this way, you will have to match his guile with a little careful thinking of your own. One way of establishing a buyer's sincerity to place business with you is to put his protestations to the test.

When a customer, having been quoted a reasonable price for the quality and quantity involved, demands a lower price as an inducement to make the change, it would be unwise to make any better offer until all other possible barriers to the acceptance of your product have been removed. Otherwise you may even get as far as quoting your rock-bottom price, confident that it will clinch the sale, only to learn subsequently that the customer has some previously undisclosed reservations about the technical acceptability of your product. This particular hurdle may take some days or weeks to overcome. By then, some further, apparently unforeseen, change has taken place in the commercial sphere and the negotiations start again—from the rock-bottom price already quoted!

The only way to deal with this kind of situation is to obtain a full and thorough evaluation of the technical merits of your product before a final negotiation on price takes place. If the customer is genuine in his desire to do business with you, he will accept the expense and trouble of approving your product before he attempts to close the deal on price.

CHAPTER ELEVEN

HOW TO ENSURE
REPEAT BUSINESS FROM YOUR CUSTOMERS

Once you have obtained the customer's business, your task will be to retain it. No longer on the attack, you will have to defend that which you have won. In many ways the defensive position is the more difficult. When you are on the attack you can to some extent choose the field of battle and the weapons you employ. As a defender, however, battlefield and weapons are often decided by persons and events outside your control.

The moment your company acquires a valuable piece of business, your competitors will be out to take it from you. Your vulnerable areas are price, quality and service: precisely those which you, when you were trying to get the business, sought to attack. Your competitors will seek to match or improve on your quality. They will try to discover the price at which you are supplying and may underquote you. Your only defence will be to make sure that the customer remains fully satisfied with his arrangements with your company, that your price remains competitive, your quality consistent and your delivery service up to standard.

Holding business already established demands of the salesman qualities additional to those he must possess to gain new business. The greatest of these is attention to detail. He must familiarize himself fully with the customer's orders and delivery instructions. This is something he should not leave to his sales office, however competent the staff may be. The responsibility for safeguarding established business lies with the sales representative.

Too often a salesman becomes disenchanted with the paper-work required for keeping a check on the service given to his customers. It is a strange state of affairs when one considers the amount of effort he has expended in acquiring a particular piece of business, yet the representative seldom seems to know the detail of customer orders and delivery schedules.

The Value of Repeated Calling

Many salesmen call regularly once a week or once a month on active accounts, always on the same day of the week and at a time agreed with the customer. The system has much to recommend it. Both the customer and the representative's office know when the visit is being made and any queries which have arisen can be prepared ready for discussion. This regularity of the salesman's calls gives the customer confidence in the organization which is supplying him.

We have previously discussed the need to apportion calls between the pursuit of new business and the servicing of existing accounts. It is obvious folly to devote so much of one's time to new business that existing business is neglected.

The Principle of Two-way Representation

The role of the sales representative is twofold. He must represent his company to its customers and potential customers. Equally, he must represent his customers to his company. Just as he is the company's ambassador, so he is also the envoy of the customers in his territory and is charged with communicating to his management their points of view on any issues which may arise. It is important that you should understand this latter role and that your customers should be aware that it exists and can benefit from it.

The representative, as an ambassador, has access to both the customer's personnel and the management personnel of his own company. If he fails to pass to his management the customer's views, even (or, indeed, especially) if they are likely to be ill-received, he is breaking the line of communication between the two parties.

It is of course necessary for him not only to report but also to interpret the customer's point of view. Where a major clash of interests occurs between company and customer, it is often due to failure on the part of the representative to explain to his management the motivations of the customer. Only by understanding thoroughly his customer's business can this dual representation be maintained. Only by regular visits will the salesman gain this understanding of his customer's needs and problems and how these are likely to be affected by the activities and the policies of his own company.

How to Ensure that Service is Maintained

By a diligent keeping of records the sales representative should know every order the customer places, the quantity, grade or quality that is required and the date on which delivery is expected. He should make it his business to see that the delivery date is kept. If he has any reason to doubt the ability of his firm to satisfy the requirements of the order, he should discuss the matter with his sales office. If a delivery is likely to be delayed for any reason, he must ensure that the customer is notified as soon as possible.

He should check regularly with the customer that the quality of his product continues to be satisfactory, that the customer's needs have remained constant and that no modification is necessary to the quality of the product to maintain his satisfaction.

If the customer has cause for complaint regarding either quality or service, the representative should deal with it immediately by personal intervention. He should not leave the problem to be sorted out by his sales-office staff. He must regard all business coming from his territory as 'his' business. Anything which may be detrimental to his company's relationship with the customers in his area is detrimental to him personally. The customer should be made to feel that the representative is close at hand at all times, ready to stand at his side and help him should problems arise.

Such close liaison, such close identity with the customer and his interests, will ensure that every problem is handled with delicacy and discretion. It will act as a counterbalance to any bungling which even in the best run companies, can occur when sales-office staff are not sufficiently attuned to the customer's viewpoint.

How to Make it Easy for the Customer to Keep His Business with Your Company

Making it easy for the customer to continue to deal with your company is the best way to ensure repeat business. Buyers, as I have said so many times already, are human. They have all the human frailties, including a desire to avoid unnecessary effort. Again, I imply no criticism; I am merely stating the obvious. Why should a buyer have to make an effort to keep buying from your firm when he has alternative suppliers who are ready and able to satisfy his requirements at less trouble to himself?

The supplier who creates unnecessary difficulties for his customer places himself in a vulnerable position, especially in a highly competitive market.

Problems of one kind or another are bound to occur between customer and supplier. They are likely to be all the greater if the product is of a sophisticated nature or the customer's particular needs are exacting. Deliveries may be late for any one of a dozen reasons. Quality may vary. Industrial firms who never encounter difficulties in securing their supplies promptly and without complaint must be so rare as to be virtually non-existent. No reasonable buyer can expect his supplies situation to run smoothly all the time. It is not that he has cause for complaint that will upset him so much as the frequency with which he has such cause. It is all a question of confidence. If he feels confident that his supplier always takes reasonable care to deliver his goods on time and to a consistent quality, and that the supplier's representative does his best to ensure that this good record is maintained, he will regard an occasional lapse as the exception rather than the rule.

When a competitor comes along, as come he will, offering a better quality or a better price, the customer will straight away call in his supplier's representative and warn him that his competitive position is under attack. He will go out of his way to provide as much information as possible to help his current supplier meet the competition. Very often he will reject the blandishments of the competitor, preferring to stay with his current supplier and to buy at a higher price than he knows he can get elsewhere, because he also knows from experience that the current supplier's service and reliability are second to none.

The maintenance of a high degree of service is a supplier's strongest safeguard against competition. His customers recognize that, in the long run, the assurance of prompt deliveries and dependable quality outweighs any marginal saving in price.

CHAPTER TWELVE

HOW TO PRESENT YOURSELF TO YOUR COMPANY

The manner in which the salesman presents himself to his company obviously has a bearing on the degree of confidence which his management places in him, and hence a bearing on his future prospects with his firm. It is important for any employee to stand well in the eyes of his colleagues and his superiors, but the image a sales representative creates has a direct influence on the effectiveness with which he can do his job.

The salesman is the eyes and ears of his management. Their interpretation of the market situation, so far as his particular area is concerned, must depend to a very large extent on the picture which he paints for them by means of his verbal and written reports. Their assessment of the company's competitive position and the acceptability of the company's products and service will be influenced to a considerable degree by the information and the comment which he passes back to them from the field. Their assessment of the value of individual items of potential business will also be coloured by the conclusions which he, with his first-hand knowledge of the account and of the customer's personnel, has reached.

One of the biggest difficulties which the area representative has in industrial selling is to 'carry his own company with him' in his negotiations with his customers. Opportunities for business which may be fully apparent to him may be disregarded by his own management. Difficulties which he can see are looming with particular customers may be dismissed as of little consequence by head-office personnel hundreds of miles away from the scene of the problem.

In an earlier chapter we saw how, in order to establish new business with a customer whose requirements are exacting, it may be necessary to develop a special quality of the product or to provide special facilities, such as the holding of certain minimum stocks, or to provide special credit arrangements. In each of these cases, the sales representative needs a degree of influence with those members of his management personnel who are responsible for deciding such matters. Much of what has previously been said in this book about the establishment of confidence has applied to the salesman/customer relationship. It is equally important that the salesman should also enjoy the confidence of his company management.

Why do people have confidence in an individual? Is it because he is dependable, reliable, knows what he is talking about? Is it because they believe that he will act responsibly, will not say one thing and do another? Is it because he is honest and not afraid to speak the truth, even though at times it may be hard or unpleasant for him to do so? If these are the reasons, perhaps they can be best summed up by the statement that people place confidence in a man who has certain minimum standards, which he applies to all that he has to do. Once they know the man they know the standards by which he lives and by which he works. The maintenance of these standards establishes his reputation: if his standards are high and he maintains them, his reputation also will be high. It is the sales representative's reputation which will be the yardstick by which his statements will be judged when he reports to his management.

The salesman who has a reputation for being a little gullible in his assessment of his customers will find it harder to impress upon his sales manager the need to take certain action than will the man with a reputation for astuteness. The representative with a reputation for accuracy will have his reports accorded greater weight than those of his colleagues with a reputation for making snap judgments.

The most important attribute which a sales manager looks for in a salesman is, or should be, the application of care and intelligence. There are many young sales representatives who possess a natural charm and a most persuasive tongue, who have a flair for getting on well with their customers, but who fail to achieve the best results simply because they do not carry with them the confidence of their sales management. Salesmen are often, and rightly, accorded the status of the 'star turns' of the sales organization. But the really effective representative is the one who combines this 'star-quality' with an ability to understand the other side of sales work: precision, attention to detail and a strong sense of responsibility.

Customers' Man or Company's Man?

The salesman must seek to identify himself closely with the interests of his customers, he must understand the motivations of the buyers and works managers of client firms and be willing and able to speak on their behalf to his own management. In pursuing the principle of two-way representation, it is his duty to assume the role of the customers' advocate to bring home to the decision-makers within his own company the viewpoint of those who control the purchasing arrangements of client firms.

There is, however, a danger here for the unwary. This close identity with his customers' interests can result in the salesman becoming identified as a 'customers' man'. It is a reputation all too easy to acquire and can lead to friction between the salesman and his sales-office staff and mark him as suspect in the eyes of his management.

A 'customers' man' is one who is prepared to see only the customers' viewpoint. So orientated has he become towards his customers' view that he can no longer appreciate the motivations of his own company. He is frequently aggressive in his attitude towards his sales office and his factory with regard to the degree of quality and service provided for his customers. He is prejudiced in his assessment of the importance of his own accounts and gains a reputation for exaggeration, both of the prescience of his customers and the short-sightedness of his own management. Being labelled a 'customers' man' implies that there is a barrier between oneself and one's own organization.

The 'customers' man' never enjoys the full confidence of his company's decision-makers because they suspect that his view is a prejudiced one. They will tend to dismiss his assessments and suggestions as biased. He will get less support than his cause may deserve and his effectiveness as a go-between will become increasingly stultified.

There is an equal danger of being purely a 'company's man': one who is over-influenced by the interests of his management's current policies. The 'company's man' will tend to play it safe, avoid seeking concessions for his customers, avoid making an issue of his company's failings in the quality and service which it provides for his customers. He will be so anxious to conform to the wishes of his management by pursuing their policies, regardless of the possible damage these might do to the business in his area, that he will fail to tell them the unpalatable truth when the occasion demands it. Because it has been denied a true picture of the market's reactions to its policies, his company will enjoy a totally false sense of security from which it is rudely awakened when at last the real facts emerge.

Maintaining the Principle of Two-way Representation

To maintain the principle of two-way representation the salesman must be prepared to be an individualist, leaning neither too far towards his customers nor too far towards his company. It requires a certain strength of character and an ability to see more than one side of the problems which arise in the customer/supplier relationship. Again, one must stress the importance of the professional attitude of mind. The professional salesman offers to his customers his services as their unpaid agent in their dealings with his firm. His function is to create business between the two, to their mutual benefit and satisfaction. But, because he is remunerated by the company which retains him, his ultimate loyalty is to that company. As he is professionally responsible for the conduct of the business between the parties, he has a right and a duty to ensure that it is conducted in such a manner that it will remain of mutual advantage to both parties.

Positive Attitudes versus Negative Attitudes

In presenting oneself to one's company, it is important to acquire a positive approach. I do not suggest that you should necessarily agree with everything that your management proposes, for even sales managers are fallible. It is your duty to oppose policies which you consider detrimental to your company's interests if applied to the customers in your care. No manager wants a 'yes-man' for a salesman.

On the other hand, nothing is more frustrating to a sales manager than to be faced with a negative attitude on the part of the sales representative. There are times when, for good or ill, certain policies have to be laid down by the management for the overall benefit of the company, the application of which may create difficulties with certain customers. Such policy decisions may include changes in the firm's range of products, in the quality of those products, in their price or in methods of packing and distribution. All such changes inevitably bring problems for some customers. It is natural for the salesman to view with suspicion anything which might place him in a position of possible disadvantage with his customers. To oppose change from a negative standpoint is, however, to fail your own management. By all means question such changes, even try to modify them. If you have serious misgivings, then oppose them; but do so positively, with an attempt to understand the reason why such changes have been proposed. If your management wish to enforce the changes as a means of overcoming certain difficulties you should at least temper your opposition with the suggestion of an alternative remedy.

The Sales Conference

Most companies hold regular meetings at which the sales management and the sales representatives sit down together to discuss the progress of their business and their future plans. Such gatherings are always fascinating because all those present are professional talkers. Every salesman earns his living by talking to his customers. But the good salesman must be more than a good talker: he must be an equally good listener.

Experienced sales managers know this. Not the least value of the sales conference is the opportunity it affords them to observe, at close quarters, the attitudes and temperament of individual salesmen.

Inevitably there will be those who will attempt to dominate the conversation. If the meeting is chaired with firmness, the compulsive talkers will be kept in check. A good chairman will seek the participation of the more reticent and, by so doing, will often enrich the discussion. The salesman who generally prefers to listen at sales meetings rather than to talk will often have more to contribute, when he does speak, than his more voluble colleagues. Indeed, the quality of a sales force may be judged to a considerable extent by the quality of the discussion which takes place at its meetings.

The main purpose of a sales conference is the exchange of information and opinion. Its success will depend, therefore, on the value of the facts and views which are presented. In approaching such a meeting, one should have a clear understanding of its aims; these may be summarized, generally, as follows.

(a) *To enable the management to inform the sales force.* Salesmen need to be brought up to date on: (i) the current situation of the company and of the industry as the management sees it, (ii) any policy changes and (iii) any new products or new markets.

(b) *To enable the salesmen to inform the management.* Management personnel need to be brought up to date on: (i) the acceptability in the field of the company, its policies and its products, (ii) market trends and (iii) any prospects of increasing the company's turnover and profitability.

The contribution one makes when speaking at sales meetings should be appropriate to the subject under discussion and to the bearing that subject may have on one's own sphere of responsibility. The salesman should be prepared to express an opinion on any of the following items: (a) the competitiveness of the company, (b) the competitiveness of the product, (c) activities of competitors, (d) market trends within his area, (e) how business can be extended and made more profitable.

Whenever you have occasion to attend a sales meeting you should try to bear these five main issues in mind. If you have prepared yourself beforehand by some clear thinking on each item, the contribution which you are able to make to the general discussion will have the merit of being appropriate and well considered; you will thereby enhance your repute within your company. Let us examine each item in detail.

(a) *The Competitiveness of the Company*
Under this heading, you may include:

(i) The *reception* of the company by your customers, i.e. its 'image'.

(ii) The *service* which the company provides for the customers within your area; whether this is adequate or inadequate, why you consider it so and how you think it can be improved.

(iii) The *sales aids* which the company provides, such as literature, samples, advertising, attendance at exhibitions and other promotions. Are these adequate and appropriate in assisting you in your sales work?

(iv) The *credit arrangements* provided for your customers. Do you consider them realistic? Are the company's credit arrangements a hindrance to the acquisition of more business?

(b) The Competitiveness of the Product
The following are some of the points to be considered:

(i) Whether the current quality is satisfactory; if not, what improvements you wish to see.

(ii) The number and type of complaints made by your customers.

(iii) What new products you believe should be added to the range and which existing items should be withdrawn.

(iv) How the prices of your product compare with those of your competitors.

(c) The Activities of Competitors
These may be summarized under two headings:

(i) How effective are they within your area? (Remember the question of attributes and limitations.)

(ii) Have there been any apparent changes in the policies pursued by your competitors in your area?

(d) Market Trends
These will be based on your own observations coupled with the views and comments expressed to you by your customers:

(i) Whether business is slack, good or very good.

(ii) Your opinion of the future pattern which business will take from the point of view of both quality and quantity.

(iii) Whether you think that prices will ease or harden.

(e) How Business can be Extended in Your Area
This is a question of your future selling plans and your assessment of the scope which exists for further business:

(i) New business you believe you can acquire. What special support, if any, will you need to accomplish it?

(ii) What increased profitability can you achieve for the company by seeking more rewarding business and relinquishing the less profitable?

Providing you have done your homework on these subjects, and therefore know what you are talking about, you should be able to make a useful contribution to their discussion. Remember that when you are invited to express your views at a sales meeting you should be prepared to tell your management what you think it needs to know, not what you think it wants to hear. To adopt a sycophantic position on what may be a controversial subject is to insult the intelligence of your superiors. Good managers not only need to know, but wish to know, the honest views of their salesmen on the policies they hope to pursue. They may not necessarily accept a contrary opinion but they will wish to hear it nevertheless, especially if it is based on accurate knowledge and sound thinking.

CHAPTER THIRTEEN

HOW TO WIN THE SUPPORT OF
SALES OFFICE AND FACTORY

There is one major difference between selling across the counter in a retail store and selling to industry. From the moment the customer walks into the shop until the moment he walks out with a neatly wrapped purchase under his arm, the entire transaction has probably been handled by one sales assistant. When the industrial sales representative transacts business with a customer, a very different situation exists.

In a shop, the sales assistant has the finished goods to hand. The quality is already established. The customer can see what he is getting. He can inspect and approve before he makes his purchase. When one is selling to industry, there can be delays while samples are made and dispatched to the customer. Very often the sample has to be subjected to some processing operation in the customer's factory before a decision can be made. If the product is sophisticated and the processing conditions are critical, a technician may have to accompany the sales representative to give special advice and assistance to the customer.

The goods which the retail customer buys are usually those which he has actually seen and approved in the shop. Goods sold to industry are manufactured, very often, only after the order has been placed. The acceptability of the quality of the goods actually supplied will not be known finally until they have been delivered and have been processed by the customer.

In the retail shop, the sales assistant takes the goods from stock, wraps them and hands the parcel to his customer, receives payment and gives change. The industrial sales representative, however, must rely on a team of other people to ensure that his transactions are properly completed. The order clerk at head office will receive the customer's order and, having checked it and had it approved for credit, will pass it on to be fitted into the factory's production programme. After the goods have been manufactured, they will be inspected, then packed and delivered. Finally, it will be the function of the accounts department to invoice the goods and to obtain payment.

Whereas the retail sales assistant is largely self-sufficient, the industrial representative is one of a team. How he gets on with the other members of this team can have a vital bearing on his effectiveness as a salesman.

The Salesman is no Stronger than the Service which Supports Him

However proficient a salesman may become in his negotiations with his customers, his ultimate effectiveness will be no stronger than the service which supports him. This is a factor which sales representatives are not always prepared to recognize. When things go wrong and opportunities are lost because of sample delays, because orders are held up or the wrong instructions have been passed to the factory, representatives are quick to blame their sales-office staff for having lost them the chance of getting additional business. When all goes well, however, and a satisfied customer not only places a first order but also repeats again and again, the salesman concerned will usually congratulate himself on a job well done and forget the part played by others in his team.

If you hope to be persistently successful in your work as a sales representative, you must not forget the others in your team. You may have the leading part to play, the 'star role', but the customer will judge the performance as a whole; and if your supporting cast is not with you, the entire show can be ruined.

The Right Attitude Towards Sales-Office Personnel

In most industrial companies the sales representative has to rely on the sales and order clerks and the typing staff for the bulk of his routine support work. While the actual division of duties will vary from one office to another, the activities of the personnel concerned may be generally summarized as follows.

(a) Sales Correspondence Clerks

Their duties usually comprise the handling of all routine correspondence with customers, such as preparing quotations, writing letters in reply to general inquiries, confirming the dispatch of samples and answering customers' telephone calls. As the 'voice at the other end of the phone', these sales clerks often play a vital role in the customer/company relationship. Those with aptitude and experience frequently become excellent 'telephone salesmen', creating and maintaining a close bond of goodwill with customers.

(b) Order Clerks

Where a separate order section is maintained within the sales office, it is the responsibility of the order clerks to process customers' orders for submission to the programming and planning sections of the factory. As soon as it is received from a customer, an order must be scrutinized to ensure that all the necessary information required by the factory is included. It has to be priced and payment arrangements checked. If the materials or components ordered are in stock, instructions must be prepared for the warehouse staff. If the goods require manufacture, dates for production and dispatch will need to be agreed with the programming personnel.

(c) Production Planning Clerks

In some firms the programming of the production of customers' orders is a function of the sales department, in others it is incorporated into the production planning operation within the factory. Whatever the system, a stage is reached in the transmission of orders from the sales office to the production floor when each order must be fitted into a programme or sequence of priorities. This is the responsibility of the programming or planning sections.

When seeking to adopt the right attitude to sales-office clerical personnel, remember that their work, in the main, is paper-work. Each clerk is likely to have a fairly well defined routine which has been laid down and which he must follow when dealing with a variety of documents. If you wish to win his support, you should try to ensure that the work you present to him has been prepared in such a manner that it fits happily into the established routine. It is obvious that the clerical staff will appreciate the salesman who sends in orders which contain all the relevant information and state precisely the quantity, quality, price, delivery date and delivery address. When he asks for samples, the thoughtful salesman always quotes the correct reference coding and states clearly to whom they are to be sent.

Sales-office staff help the salesmen who help themselves. They do not appreciate being asked to correct mistakes and omissions which are the result of carelessness or laziness on the part of the representative.

Do not be over-demanding of your sales-office resources. It is a mistake to try to get an unfair share of priorities for all your customers all the time. If you avoid making unnecessary demands you will find the staff more prepared to ensure that you receive adequate service at all times. You should always be prepared to assist the office staff in dealing with customer problems, however trivial. Any problem they have with a customer in your territory is your problem, too. The care of the customers in your area is your responsibility.

Do not try to 'bend' the rules laid down regarding delivery priorities in order to satisfy unreasonable demands from customers. If the delivery arrangements are inadequate, take the matter up with your sales manager. Do not throw your weight about with the order clerk to pressurize him into giving your customers priority treatment. If priority is really necessary in the company's interest, the correct approach is to the sales manager.

The Right Attitude Towards Technical Personnel

There are occasions when it is necessary to involve technical personnel in sales work, especially if the products to be sold are of a sophisticated nature. Technical assistance can be useful in providing advice to customers generally and is often essential when one is investigating quality complaints. The sales representative needs to win the willing support of his technical personnel; they can, very often, help him considerably to increase his sales.

It must be remembered that technically minded people are seldom sales-orientated. One should not expect them to view a situation in the same light as a commercially trained person. Salesmanship is not their function. Their motivations will be different from yours. When you take a technician to investigate a customer's problem, your main preoccupation will be to safeguard your existing business with that account and to seek every opportunity to extend your sales. The technical man, however, approaches the situation from a different standpoint. First and foremost in his mind is the need to understand the exact nature of the problem. It may prove to be an intrinsically interesting problem from a purely technical point of view. The problem will be a personal challenge to him, to his training and expertise. Whereas you will merely wish to have it solved so that you can resume your commercial progress with the customer, he may wish to dwell on it at length, not merely to resolve this specific difficulty but because, for him, there is this intrinsic interest and fascination.

Technically minded people tend to be less objective than commercial people. They have a thirst for knowledge for its own sake and can become avidly preoccupied in the solution of problems which, from the purely commercial point of view, are of limited importance. This is not said to underrate the technician upon whom, after all, the salesman must depend for the conception, design and production of the goods which he is employed to sell. The more sophisticated the product, the more technical knowledge and expertise there will be behind it. In modern industry the scientist and the salesman are mutually dependent. Their motivations, however, can be very different. By understanding this difference and the reasons for it, one can appreciate the attitude of mind of one's technical colleagues and thus maintain harmonious relations with them.

The best help which the salesman can give to his technical staff is to feed them with as much information as possible regarding customers' processing methods and any problems which may arise in the use of the company's products. The worst that you can do is to try to teach them their job. It is not uncommon to find a salesman, who has picked up a smattering of technical knowledge about the products which he handles, attempting to tell the qualified technical man how he should approach a technical problem. Technicians who have spent many years acquiring their qualifications are naturally contemptuous of the meddling amateur, they will have no respect for the sales representative who affects a spurious understanding of technicalities which, in any event, lie outside his province.

When to Seek the Help of Your Sales Manager

It is a mistake to try to deal with all customer problems on your own. I have already pointed out that industrial selling is team-work. The salesman should never be afraid to ask for the assistance of others if a situation arises which he does not feel qualified to handle unaided. A problem shared is a problem halved, and many issues which arise in sales work can be resolved more quickly if you call in the help of other members of your team rather than try to battle it out alone.

Consultation with your sales manager is a vital first step in dealing with a difficult situation. From his greater knowledge and experience he may well be able to suggest a line of approach which you have not considered. If the importance of the customer warrants it, he may decide to make a joint visit with you to discuss the matter at first hand. There are certain customers who may not wish to deal with a young representative, but who will be willing to talk to a more senior person. They will wish to be assured that what they have to say will get through to the company's management. A customer may consider that what is your best offer may not, in fact, be the best offer which he can get from your company, whereas he will probably accept that price as final when it is quoted to him by the sales manager. You may be faced with an account problem where some modification to your firm's policy is necessary to accommodate a specific customer. Very often a situation of this kind can be settled promptly by a personal visit of your sales manager.

CHAPTER FOURTEEN

RECORD-KEEPING

The Problem of 'Bumf'

One of the problems of modern business is the accumulation of an ever-growing mass of paper which, unless it is controlled, clogs the administrative machine. It is to be hoped that the firm for whom you work will have a sensible attitude and will not attempt to overburden their representatives with too much 'bumf'.

There are, however, certain essential records which you will need to keep to enable you to carry out your duties efficiently. The art of dealing with paper-work is to discriminate between that which is to be read and discarded immediately and that which must be retained for future reference. The undiscriminating salesman stuffs every piece of paper he receives from his office into folders and carries them about with him until he can physically accommodate no more. He then has a big turnout and a bonfire in his garden. Very often, he finds that he cannot lay his hands on the one sheet of paper he really needs because it is lost in the general mass of irrelevant documents.

A far better method is to destroy practically every copy-letter, quotation and copy-order after you have read it and after you have extracted the essential details. These extractions should be entered into a customers' record system. To do this demands the setting aside of time, on a daily basis, purely for record-keeping.

There will be those who will object to this proposal on the grounds that a salesman's job is to sell, not to set himself up as a glorified clerk. However, if one accepts the need for some essential records, the system possesses two particular merits: (*a*) it avoids the accumulation of sheets of paper, which can be the bane of a sales representative's life; (*b*) it ensures that the extracted information is the very minimum necessary to enable you to run your territory—you will have neither the time nor the desire to note down anything other than that which you consider is essential.

Some Suggested Equipment

The office-equipment industry can offer practically every method of recording and storing written information, and it is not my intention to list the variety of files, folders, card-index systems and the like which are available for these purposes.

Whatever equipment you choose should be portable. Some representatives like to work with card indexes rather than loose-leaf books. The objection to this is that they are not so easy to carry about and the weight of 100 cards in a box is far greater than that of 100 sheets of paper in a loose-leaf binder. It may be argued that, since the majority of industrial salesmen have motor-cars, the question of bulk and weight does not apply. Files and card-indexes will, however, have to be taken to and from the car and the house each day. Furthermore, there are days when the car is being serviced or for some other reason is not available. Then the unwieldy filing system becomes a curse, whereas the handy-sized loose-leaf book can be carried easily in a brief-case.

The Minimum Records You Require

The minimum records which you need in servicing your accounts and in seeking new business are as follows:

(*a*) *Customers' Address Book* for recording the names, addresses and telephone numbers of the customers in your area, together with the names of the individuals whom one needs to contact. In this book you should also include any specially relevant information such as (i) the days of the week when your contact prefers not to see visitors and (ii) customers' holiday dates.

(*b*) *Customers' Order Record*. Some method of recording customers' orders is essential. One of the simplest is a loose-leaf binder with a page inserted for each customer. In addition to the customer's name, the page should be subdivided to provide for entries to be made under the following headings:

Date of order
Customer's order number
Your order number
Quantity
Colour
Grade or quality reference
Price
Delivery-required date
Delivery quoted
Date of dispatch
Quantity dispatched
Special remarks

If the customers' sheets are placed in the book alphabetically, the information can be easily entered from the copy-orders sent to you by your sales office. Whenever you are visiting a customer you will have at hand a complete record of the business he has placed with you over previous months and you will be able to see at a glance which of his orders is outstanding at any particular time.

This form of record also provides you with the pattern of customer's orders. By comparing, month by month, the frequency with which items are reordered, you will be able to see when a new order is due and also spot those that are overdue.

(*c*) *Business Opportunities Record.* You will need some means of keeping track of new-business opportunities at each account or potential account. A very simple system is to use for this purpose a copy of your last visit report. If it contains any matters which were not included in the report actually submitted to your management, add a note to this effect. When you next call on the customer in question, you have merely to take from the file the last report copy and you have all the information so far gleaned about a new project. Later, a copy of the report on the current call will go into the file and the previous copy can then be destroyed.

Every salesman eventually devises a personal record system to suit his own working methods. Whatever system you adopt, the essential requirements are that it should be as condensed as possible, should take the minimum amount of time and effort to maintain and yet provide all the really essential information needed to allow the salesman to do his job properly.

CHAPTER FIFTEEN

HOW TO DEAL WITH DIFFICULT CUSTOMERS

Every sales area has its crop of difficult customers. Every company knows particular firms where it has tried again and again to get business, without success. When you start out on the road, you too will come across customers whom you will label as 'difficult' and you may decide to devote your efforts towards other accounts where business seems more likely to be obtained.

Sooner or later, however, you will be looking back over your shoulder at those 'difficult' customers with the knowledge that they are offering you a challenge. In fact, the more you are told by colleagues and members of your senior management that you will never break in *there*, the more determined you will become to prove them wrong.

In general conversation, 'a difficult customer' means an individual who is not easy to get along with. He may be exacting in what he expects of others. He may be reticent in showing his feelings. He may be unbending, not easily swayed. Often we hear it said of such a person that 'he's all right when you get to know him'.

As with people in ordinary life, so with customers. You have to try to understand the customer's motives. You have to ask yourself why he appears 'difficult'. Is it because he asks too much of his suppliers? He may be doing a good buying job by expecting the best value for his company's money. Is it because he does not make life easy for the salesman or the order clerk? There is no reason why he should. He is not asking you to supply him. If you want his business, he will expect you to do things the way he wants them done.

A customer only proves 'difficult' to a supplier whose salesmanship, products, service or selling price is inadequate. Providing you can give him adequate facilities, he will not appear to you to be so difficult. He may be exacting, but this will only be in comparison with your other customers.

He may be 'difficult' in the sense that he is hard on sales people: bullying, complaining, sarcastic. These, however, are merely the personal failings of the individual. If your shortcomings are such that you give him cause to bully or complain or be sarcastic, then you must expect such treatment from such a person. Providing you can meet his needs and go on meeting them better than any of your competitors, he must buy from you. He may always be a tiresome man to have to deal with, but so is the easy-going buyer who never knows what he wants and when he wants it. If selling was not difficult, anyone could do your job: you cannot have it both ways.

Analysing the Difficult Customer

If you are determined to sell to the 'difficult' customer, it is as well to define the term. Such a customer is:

(*a*) One who will not buy from you.
(*b*) One who is willing to buy from you but only on conditions which it is difficult to fulfil.
(*c*) One whose demands are exacting.

There may be other definitions, but these will cover the majority of situations.

To understand why a customer is 'difficult', we need to examine each of the above definitions in some detail.

(*a*) *The Customer Who Will Not Buy From You*

Let us consider the most likely reasons why a customer should refuse to buy.

(i) *Your service/product/price is not competitive.* If this is true, then it is up to you to get your company to make itself competitive so far as this particular account is concerned. If there are good reasons why it cannot do so, then you should make it clear to your management that they must accept the fact that this piece of business is outside the scope of the company's market.

(ii) *The customer has an association of long standing with his current supplier.* Unseating a long-established competitor is always difficult. No company exists merely to buy materials or components. It buys in goods to process and sell and make a profit for its shareholders. Buyers are not employed, primarily, to find alternative sources of supply for these goods. They know that to change suppliers is an undertaking not without risk. Often it is costly. For a buyer to chop and change his sources of supply could be regarded as a criticism of his buying strategy; it suggests that his previous choice of supplier was a mistake. To change from one supplier to another because the buyer prefers one salesman to another is not a justifiable reason. There must be an advantage. Very often customers earn the reputation of being 'difficult' simply because they have no wish to change from their current supplier. More precisely, they have no *reason* to wish to change.

(iii) *The customer is prejudiced.* A customer with a prejudice against a potential supplier is certainly 'difficult'. His prejudice may stem from any one of a number of causes. It may be based on dislike or distrust of the salesman, the company's management, its trading policies, the quality of its products or the reliability of its service.

The most important factor in any good business relationship is confidence, which is based on trust. If the customer feels that he cannot trust the supplier to give him a fair deal, he will not have the confidence to place business with him. The salesman's task is to create confidence or, where mistrust exists, to try to recreate confidence.

You should explore every opportunity to build confidence. Be prepared to accept even the smallest order as a means of reassuring the customer that your quality is acceptable and your delivery service is satisfactory. Ensure that any quotations or samples submitted arrive within the time promised. Ask your sales manager to back you by insisting that every action which your company takes in connection with this account is prompt and accurate.

(iv) *Inertia.* There are customers who will delay the decision to give business to a potential supplier, not because they have any real objections to doing so, but out of inertia. It is always easier to 'leave things as they are' and, in any case, a change of supply source is a hazard. A buyer will postpone making a change even though he knows he is being offered a better price or a better quality. He claims to be too busy or imagines that the time is not quite right.

There is only one answer to this situation: keep up the pressure by persistent calling.

(b) *The Customer Who Imposes Difficult Conditions*

Before you label a customer as 'difficult' because he seeks to impose difficult conditions, you should first look at your competitiveness. If a customer can afford to impose conditions which you and your company consider difficult, it is because he can find alternative sources where his conditions are met. At least one of your competitors must, seemingly, be able and willing to give him all that he asks.

It does not necessarily follow that it will be in the interests of your company to fall in with whatever a competitor is doing. Your firm may be in the fortunate position of being able to sell the bulk of its output under conditions which it deems to be reasonable. If so, there is little merit in taking on a commitment with a customer on unreasonable terms. The truth of the matter may be that the competitor is not as well placed as your company and is prepared to go to excessive lengths to obtain business which could prove of doubtful value to him in the long run.

(c) *The Customer Whose Demands Are Exacting*

It is well known that the customer to whom it is difficult to sell often proves, once the business has been gained, one of the least easy to lose. Providing he is satisfied with his current supplier, the exacting customer is far from willing to change to a competitive source. Such a customer is not, in fact, as 'difficult' as one might imagine. One of the problems of dealing with an apparently 'easy' customer is that, very often, he does not really know what he wants. The exacting customer, on the other hand, knows exactly what he wants, states his requirements clearly and thereby makes it easier for his supplier to satisfy him.

Some Approaches which Lead to Progress

Your chances of getting business at a difficult account should always be put to the test very thoroughly before you give up and decide to devote your efforts to easier targets. The difficult customer is a challenge and there is more satisfaction to be gained from getting business from one difficult account than three easy ones. Such business, once gained, is often easier to hold.

Make it evident to the difficult buyer that, far from being put off, you are determined to win his business. Maintain regular calls. He will soon come to realize that you are one of those people who, having set your mind to achieve something, will not give up until you have succeeded. Regular calling will also give you the opportunity of really getting to know the man you are dealing with.

Try to get him to come out of his office or his factory. Suggest to him that he should join you for lunch, or, better still, for dinner. A change of venue can work miracles.

Another useful way of breaking down prejudice in a customer is to ask him if he would like to visit your factory to see for himself how your products are made. If he accepts, make sure that you do the thing properly. Pick him up by car and, on arrival at the factory, invite him to have coffee in the works manager's office. This can be followed by a quick tour of the plant, probably under the guidance of the works manager or some other senior member of the production staff, followed by a pleasant lunch. In the afternoon, encourage him to see again anything which is of special interest to him, not forgetting your quality-control department and your packing and dispatch sections. In going round the site he will have met a number of your technical and production personnel. He will have got the feeling that he *knows* your firm. Whenever you call to see him in the future, he will be reminded of all that he has seen. He will have far greater confidence in what you have to tell him simply because he has seen it for himself.

The next stage in building the confidence of the difficult customer is to find an opportunity of proving your quality, your service and your general reliability. If the customer is using a product in regular quantities and you have a quality similar to that supplied by your competitor, ask him to put through a trial run with your material. Be prepared to supply it on a sale-or-return basis without any 'strings'.

Playing the Waiting Game

All business situations are subject to constant change. In a previous chapter I spoke of the fluctuating fortunes of business firms; of their rise, their period of eminence and their period of decline. Shakespeare reminds us that there is a tide in the affairs of men. There is a tide, too, in the affairs of businesses, and that which may seem impossible one day can appear almost inevitable at a later date, sometimes years later.

No customer/supplier situation remains unchanged for ever. The customer who will not look at your product and your company now, for any one of a dozen good reasons, may well sing a different tune in two or three years' time. That may seem a long while to wait if you have just taken over a territory and are impatient to acquire new business. You will find, however, that the years soon pass. Within the passage of time there is a passage of events. Market needs alter, suppliers who currently appear to dominate the account may cease to be competitive in price or quality or service. The needs of the customer, reflecting the changing needs of his market, may alter. Time is often the great healer, not only of our personal problems, but also of our frustrated sales efforts.

The work which you put into trying to sell to an account today may take a very long time to bear fruit. It will never be entirely wasted, provided that you maintain continued contact. Let me offer you an example.

Suppose that you have tried very hard indeed to get your product accepted by a customer. You have submitted quotations which are very competitive, samples which have performed successfully. Yet, in spite of all these efforts, you have drawn a blank. The customer will not buy from you, although you are confident that you have done everything possible to win him over. It would be a natural reaction to decide to cut your losses and give up the struggle. You may conclude that you will never sell into this account and your time and effort could be better spent elsewhere.

Certainly your experience will have proved that you are most unlikely to get any business in the short term. You will be right to transfer the bulk of your efforts towards more promising results elsewhere. But you would be wrong to shut the door completely. If you did, you would have wasted all your previous effort. Make a point of seeing this customer at least two or three times a year. Keep the pot boiling, or at least simmering. Unless you do this, you will not know if the situation changes. The buyer who has proved so intractable may be sacked, or be promoted or transferred to another side of the business. He may go and get himself another job. You never know your luck!

In these days of rationalization, it is not uncommon for small firms to be taken over by larger ones and for large firms to amalgamate with competitors. When such things happen, policies which may previously have been viable may no longer be realistic. New men appear on the scene with a fresh approach. You may decide to write down a customer as being of little immediate prospect. You can never afford to write him off.

The Value of Multi-tier Contact with Difficult Accounts

We discussed earlier the benefits which can accrue from the occasional intervention of one's sales manager to assist the sales representative in dealing with customers on specific issues. There are some accounts, however, where it may be desirable for the sales manager, and possibly the sales director, to maintain regular contact with their opposite numbers within the client company. Such contact can augment and support the work of the salesman, who will then deal exclusively with the buyer or the works manager.

One of the advantages of this multi-tier contact with a customer is that it avoids the personality problems which can occur when the sales representative tries to establish relationships with a number of people of differing rank at a particular account. The buyer will feel no resentment that, while you call to see him, your superiors deal with his superiors. A second advantage is that the top men in the client firm have direct access to the top men in your company and the bonds between the two organizations are thereby considerably strengthened.

Finally, multi-tier contact with an established account will ensure that every point of entry by a competitor is guarded. If the only link is the salesman/buyer relation, your competitor may be able to outflank you by establishing a connection at director level. Equally, where the only point of contact with a customer is at high level, the buyers and works managers may feel that they are being left out in the cold on matters which affect their departments. They are thus easy prey for the competitor's representative, who may succeed, at shop-floor level, in getting his materials tested and approved.

The Value and Dangers of Back-selling

Many industrial products are sold to processors, i.e. firms who convert a raw material into a finished component. This component is sold by them to what may be called an 'end-user'. The plastics industry offers a good example of such a sequence. A plastics raw material in granular form is sold by the manufacturer to a moulder who converts it into, say, a motor-car facia panel, knobs for television sets or the freezer-compartment door of a refrigerator. None of these items in itself is an end-product. They are all components which the moulder in his turn sells to his customer, who may be a motor-car manufacturer, a television manufacturer or a refrigerator manufacturer. With the increasing sophistication of these industries, it is normal practice for the end-product manufacturer to lay down specifications detailing not only the shape, size and colour of the components which he buys, but also the type of material from which they are to be made. Furthermore, it is not unusual for him to conduct proving trials on individual makes of the material he requires to be used and to include in his specifications the names of the raw-material producers and the grade codings of their products which he has approved.

Where such a situation exists, it may not be sufficient for the raw-material manufacturer to sell his products only to the processor. If a moulder has a contract to produce a certain number of facia panels and a particular raw-material supplier's name does not appear on the list of approved grades, he cannot buy from that supplier for this particular application. The only recourse open to the plastics producer is to approach the motor-car manufacturer direct and persuade him to test and approve his material for the job. He then must ensure that his name and the grade coding for his material are added to the specification which is given to the moulder.

The principle of 'back-selling', as it is called, has in recent years become an accepted method of selling to industry. It must, of course, go hand in glove with direct selling to the processor. Some companies have two teams of sales representatives: those who sell to the processor and those who deal solely with the design and development divisions of the end-users.

Back-selling can create a lot of business if properly handled. It provides one avenue of approach to the problem of selling one's products into a processing firm which may not, of its own volition, be inclined to buy its raw materials from a particular source. When the buyer of a processing company finds that his sales department has obtained a contract to mould several thousand radio cabinets, for example, and your company's grade is the only one which appears on the specification, he has little option but to buy from you. He could, of course, challenge the specification and suggest an alternative material. In doing so, however, he would run the risk that the alternative which he suggests might subsequently prove to be unsuitable. Any fault which occurred in the processed product during assembly or subsequently, and which could be attributed to some failing in the raw material, would place the processor in an embarrassing position.

It will be seen that to back-sell is to circumvent the processing company's buying department. There are, however, serious dangers in adopting this strategem. Whereas a user may be content to let his supplier contact his customer with a view to getting a product specified, he is likely to object if he feels he is to be put under pressure to use a material or a component that he does not want to buy. No one likes to feel that he is being coerced, and there have been cases where very considerable ill feeling has developed between a processor and a potential supplier because the back-selling technique has been used too aggressively and without discrimination.

CHAPTER SIXTEEN

THE QUESTION OF COMPETITORS

From time to time changes occur in the type of materials and the type of components needed to meet the demands of any particular industry. These may be caused by fluctuations in the economic climate of the country, changes in social habits or changes in fashion. In any period of general economic growth, however, the overall demand for such materials and components is likely to remain continuous. Industrial firms must purchase those materials and parts which are necessary for the manufacture of their own products and they must continue to buy them in order to maintain their own production.

When you are selling to industry, therefore, your primary task may not be to induce the customer to use a particular type of raw material or a particular kind of component in his production, but to induce him buy it from you rather than from your competitor.

There are times when salesmen delude themselves that the contest in which they are engaged is between themselves and the customer. In fact the contest is between themselves and their competitor, with the customer's business as the prize to the winner.

Know Your Enemy

In order to win this contest with your competitor, it is essential to understand the strength of his position. Obviously, the more you know about his products, his marketing policies, his service to customers and the kind of people whom he employs to sell his goods, the greater will be your knowledge of his competitive merit in relation to your own.

Lord Montgomery is said to have displayed inside the caravan which he used during the El Alamein campaign, a framed photograph of Field Marshal Rommel, the commander of the German Afrika Korps. When asked about this, 'Monty' explained that he kept it in front of him because it helped him to know his enemy.

I do not suggest that you should festoon the inside of your car with snapshots of your competitor's salesmen! What I do suggest, however, is that you should try to obtain copies of your competitor's literature and price lists, study the selling features of his products, note how they are packed and transported, make a list of his major customers and assess his likely total sales in your area.

To pry into a customer's relationship and arrangements with a competitor by asking impertinent questions is, as I have said before, something which is definitely frowned upon. But customers do talk about one supplier to another and whenever this occurs you should make a mental note of anything which will increase your knowledge of your competitor's activities.

There are many industries in which the salesmen of competing companies get to know one another and are on friendly terms. They are each selling the same kind of product within the same market, they are calling on the same customers and have very similar problems. Encounters often occur at the doorways of customers' premises, at trade association meetings and at trade exhibitions.

In getting to know your enemy it is often a good idea to make a friend of him. There may be times when he will help you and you will help him. In the end, the best man wins.

An Eternal Triangle

In any selling operation, three people are involved: the buyer, the seller and the alternative supplier. Your competitor may be an unseen member of the triangle, but he is always there, conditioning both your approach and the customer's approach to the negotiations. If the competitor did not exist, trading would be merely a matter of striking a bargain between buyer and seller; the seller could offer poor quality products at an inflated price with an atrocious service and the buyer would have to accept. The existence of the competitor is an assurance that the supplier will at least try to provide the best quality he can afford at the best price, compatible with making a reasonable profit, and a service adequate for the customer's needs.

Understanding a Competitor's Motives

If you were asked what your competitor was trying to achieve, you might answer that he was trying to take away your business and that he wanted to sell as much of his product to as many customers as possible. This may not, however, be entirely true.

It should not be assumed that your competitor's manufacturing facilities, his business organization or his marketing policy is the same as that of your own company. We have already seen how the differing size of companies can result in differing competitive merit. Differences in the age of firms can account for differences in the type of plant they have installed over past years and can therefore affect their marketing strategy. A firm whose plant consists of machines of varying sizes and capacities may be capable of offering a very comprehensive service to its customers. It may be able to handle special qualities very economically. A rival firm which has installed high-speed equipment designed to manufacture a limited range of products in large quantities will be less versatile. This second firm may be able to underquote the first for long-run jobs, but could be outpriced when it comes to short-run work. The more automated a production line becomes, the less it can tolerate the manufacture of small quantities or special qualities.

As a further example, let us take the case of a competitor selling a second quality of his product into an account in considerable quantity and at a very low price. The customer may invite you to take this business, if you can match the price. Now, the process employed by your competitor may be such that, in order to achieve an acceptable first quality to meet the general demand of the market, he cannot avoid the production of a percentage of slightly substandard material or components. He must find an outlet for these 'seconds', and the customer in question provides such an outlet. By disposing of all his 'seconds' to this one customer, he ensures that he maintains an acceptable first-quality product for distribution to the rest of the trade. You may decide that, to achieve high-volume sales, you are prepared to relieve him of this particular piece of business by selling your first-quality product to this customer at his 'seconds' price. But with what result? Your competitor must still dispose of this quantity of second-quality merchandise. You are likely to find that, in desperation, he is offering it all round the trade and may be disrupting your established business with other customers.

An understanding of your competitor's motives in selling all his 'seconds' to one outlet could have prevented you from attacking him at an account where, in the long run, it was not in your interests to do so.

All manufacturing organizations are to some extent handicapped by the need for the economic utilization of their plants. Business which may seem very attractive to one supplier, because his factory is geared to handle it economically, may be of no interest to another, who knows he will lose money on it because it will not suit his production arrangements. If you can learn about your competitor's production capabilities it will help you to understand his marketing policy. In turn, this will enable you to assess your relative competitive merit with greater accuracy when you come to negotiate for a customer's business.

CHAPTER SEVENTEEN

HOW TO DEAL WITH COMPLAINTS

Every customer is liable to complain to a manufacturing company about the quality of its goods. As a sales representative you will be directly involved when a complaint arises. Let us consider, therefore, some of the reasons why complaints occur.

When one is offering a product in a competitive market, the quality of that product must be adequate to meet the customers' requirements at the price for which they are prepared to pay for it. Consider the situation which may arise with paint sold by your competitors at £1·75 per gallon. Since this is the price which paint of this quality will fetch, it is likely that £1·75 is the maximum price which your customer will be willing to pay it. The quality of the paint which you are offering, however, might be slightly superior to that of your competitors. This would appear to be excellent from your point of view, because it would give you a competitive advantage on quality.

Let us suppose, however, that this superior quality costs your company £2·00 a gallon to make. Clearly, you cannot afford to sell it at £1·75 a gallon. It will be necessary to get your chemists to arrive at a quality which will be adequate for the customer's purposes, at a cost which will show a reasonable return when sold at £1·75 per gallon.

In a highly competitive market, no supplier can maintain consistently a higher standard than is necessary for the use to which the product is to be put. Otherwise he will either need to sell it at a price which is too high to be competitive or, by selling it at the market price, he will lose money on it.

This means that the margin between what is adequate and what is inadequate must be, at times, fairly narrow. To provide a product which is neither too good nor too bad for the purpose for which it is intended, demands skill on the part of those responsible for its production. The more sophisticated the product, the greater will be the hazard that what is produced may be variable in quality.

The assessment of quality can be very difficult. If the standard to which the quality controller works is set too high, the result could be that very little of the factory's production will ever get out of the gate. Production costs will soar, deliveries will not be made and the firm will fail through self-induced strangulation. This would obviously be an absurd situation. On the other hand, if the standard is set too low, there could be a steady flow of faulty merchandise going out to customers, with equally disastrous consequences.

In practice, of course, a standard is set at a level of quality which, it is thought, the market will tolerate. In other words, the standard will be that which is considered adequate for the applications for which the product is being purchased.

In arriving at a tolerable standard, the manufacture must allow for the degree of variation which may exist in the requirements of his customers. If he fails to do so, the generally accepted standard may prove to be inadequate and a complaint will result.

There are, of course, many other reasons why complaints occur. The wrong quality may be ordered by the customer. The wrong quality may be supplied. A mistake may be made in the formulation and may not be detected during inspection. The materials or components may become damaged in packing or in transit. All such complaints will be the result of negligence on the part of somebody at some stage between the placing of the order and the delivery of the goods.

Another reason why complaints occur is that the customer misuses the product. The supplier is not responsible for how the product is used or misused, so complaints of this kind are unreasonable and should be rejected.

To summarize: a firm which never has a complaint might be setting itself a production standard which is too high to be economically justified; a firm which has too many complaints is allowing the standard of its production to be too variable and its quality-control department is not doing its job.

The Customer's Mental Attitude to a Complaint

When a customer receives a consignment of goods which he considers to be defective, he is going to be put to some inconvenience at the very least. His normal procedure of receiving the goods, taking them into stock and subsequently issuing them to his own production units is disturbed. He finds himself with a quantity of merchandise on his hands which he wants to get rid of. More particularly, he wants a replacement. He needs the goods, but they must be of the correct quality. Until he gets them he cannot continue his own production.

The customer's first reaction, then, is one of irritation. He has been put to unnecessary trouble owing to some oversight on the part of his supplier. He wants something done about it. He wants the faulty goods removed. He does not want to be charged for them, which means that if he has already received an invoice for them, he will want a credit note. He is anxious that the defective material or components should be taken out of his premises. While they are there he runs the risk that, inadvertently, they might get used in his production and he will be in even worse trouble. He wants to know when he is going to get a replacement and he wants to be assured that when the replacement arrives it will be to specification. Finally, he is seeking an assurance that there is not going to be any recurrence of this kind of mistake.

When a complaint is accepted by the supplier, he should take away the faulty goods and arrange replacement as speedily as possible.

Where the supplier does not necessarily agree that the goods are faulty the customer will usually accept the fact that before they are removed the supplier will wish to inspect them. A reasonable customer will recognize that his supplier, having incurred the costs of packing and delivery, will not wish to incur the additional expense of transportation back to his factory and the delivery of a replacement until he is sure that the complaint is justified. He will, however, expect this investigation to be carried out quickly and an early decision to be reached.

Your Company's Mental Attitude to a Complaint

The attitude of your company is likely to be one of wariness. No supplier likes to have to deal with a complaint. A complaint automatically suggests some lack of competence on the part of the production staff or quality-control personnel. There is bound to be an inquest into how this allegedly faulty batch was allowed to go out to the customer. No one likes to be accused of incompetence, and it is very natural that the first instinct is one of defence. How sure is the customer that the goods are, in fact, faulty?

There is another reason why your company may deal cautiously with a customer's complaint. If the material supplied has been used by the customer in his own production process and then found to be faulty, the machine time and labour expended on this abortive production will be a complete loss to him. Going a step further, we could have a situation where the customer converts the materials or utilizes the components he has bought in the production of a finished article. If he sells this finished article and it fails in service owing to a defect in the material or the components he has used, a claim for compensation may be made against him by *his* customer.

As an example of such a situation, consider a plastics producer who is supplying moulding compound to an injection moulder for the production of heels for ladies' shoes. If the moulding compound is below the specification as far as strength is concerned, this may not be apparent to the moulder whose uses it to produce several thousand heels. These heels are sold to a shoe manufacturer who nails them to the uppers of his shoes. Upon nailing, the heels crack. The shoe manufacturer has not only suffered the loss of the broken heels, but of ruined shoes as well, for he cannot remove the broken heels without damaging the shoes.

The shoe manufacturer would claim compensation from the moulder of the heels, not only for the cost of the heels, but also for the cost of the shoes. In his turn the moulder would pass on this claim, together with a claim for his own abortive running costs incurred in producing the heels, to the plastics manufacturer.

Suppliers are well aware of the hazards of claims being made against them in respect of the supply of faulty goods. Many of them therefore include in their Conditions of Sale a clause to the effect that they will not entertain claims for consequential loss. This provides them with a legal safeguard without which they would lay themselves open to the possibility of meeting demands for crippling amounts. However, most suppliers feel obliged to meet a legitimate claim for consequential loss in order to maintain goodwill.

Such claims can, in certain circumstances, be substantial and might wipe out the total profit earned by trading with the customer in question for months or even years. So it is understandable that company managements are often wary of admitting liability until a complaint has been investigated thoroughly.

Your Mental Attitude to a Complaint

It is never a pleasant task to have to deal with a complaint. It is, however, part of the salesman's lot. As the company's representative, it is his job to go and find out what the complaint is all about. Inevitably he is the first man to face the customer's wrath.

A customer with a complaint certainly needs careful handling. He is at least likely to be irritated, probably very annoyed, at the trouble he has been caused. Very often his annoyance is due not so much to his own inconvenience, but to the inconvenience which this faulty consignment may cause his customer. It may mean that he has to delay his deliveries and thus incur his customer's displeasure. Through no fault of his own he is going to let his own customer down.

The customer naturally wishes to express his annoyance; the sooner he can express it and thus get it off his chest, the better for the customer/supplier relationship. Unhappily, it is part of the sales representative's work to receive the blame from the customer on behalf of his company.

If the customer was rational about the matter he would accept that the salesman could be in no way personally responsible for the complaint. However, customers are often irrational on such occasions. When we sit down in a restaurant to have a meal and find that the potatoes are uncooked or the meat is cold, it is to the waiter that we complain. It is to him that we direct our dissatisfaction, although if we were rational about the matter we would realize that he has merely carried the plate from the kitchen to our table. It is the cook in the kitchen who should be the target for our annoyance.

Customers are never likely to be more justly irritated than when they are under the strain of having to meet delivery dates themselves and find that the consignment of material or components upon which they must rely is unusable.

When a complaint occurs in his territory, the salesman is placed on his mettle. The first rule is to get to the customer as quickly as possible. Nothing will annoy a customer more than to have a complaint which, apparently, nobody wants to know about. He wants to get his annoyance off his chest and wants the salesman present so that he can tell him what he thinks about his company and its products. This, then, is your first task, to act as a kind of punch-bag.

It is no good thinking how grossly unfair it is that the customer is blaming you for the shortcomings of your factory. This is where, once again, one's professionalism must show itself. It is necessary to be sympathetic to the customer's situation. One must show that one shares the customer's concern about the dislocation which this faulty batch of goods has caused to the smooth running of his factory and the possible harm it may do to his relations with his own customers.

Investigation and Correction

Having made it clear to the customer that he will do everything in his power to have matters put right as quickly as possible, the salesman should immediately begin an investigation into what needs to be done. He should establish all the necessary details concerning the faulty consignment, the date on which it was delivered, the reference number of the relevant advice or delivery note and any special markings on the packages which may assist identification. He should then examine the evidence which the customer has to substantiate the complaint and obtain samples of the allegedly faulty material or components.

The salesman who is a fair-weather friend only and is noticeable by his absence when trouble occurs will not earn his customer's respect or his confidence. Equally, the company's management can have little confidence in a representative who leaves it to the sales-office staff or the technical personnel to sort out a complaint in his territory. There may be occasions when a customer's technical problem is so complex that there seems to be little that the non-technical salesman can contribute. He should remember, however, that his presence is in itself reassuring to the customer. It implies that both he and his company are concerned about the problem and that its solution is of greater immediate importance than any other claims there might be upon his time and his effort.

A customer with a complaint on his hands is a customer in trouble. The salesman who demonstrates that he is concerned about it, and is trying to do something about it, cannot fail to earn that customer's goodwill. In the long run, the manner in which he behaves on these occasions is of greater importance than the keenness of his price or the quality of his product. Reliability, especially in a time of crisis, is the greatest recommendation in industrial salesmanship.

CHAPTER EIGHTEEN

HOW TO DEAL WITH ACCOUNT PROBLEMS

There is divided opinion on whether the handling of account problems should or should not come within the responsibility of the sales representative. Equally good arguments can be mounted for and against.

It is never pleasant to have to go and ask someone for money, to have to tell a customer that, if he does not pay his account, action will have to be taken which could begin with the stopping of further deliveries and could end in legal proceedings. Such a vexed situation could damage a salesman's personal relationship with the customer irrecoverably, and he might have the greatest difficulty in selling anything to that firm in the future.

On the other hand, there are many excellent customer/supplier relationships of long standing which would probably not have come into existence but for a timely intervention by the salesman to settle an account difficulty. The wisdom of using a sales representative to deal with an account problem depends on the capabilities of the man concerned and the kind of relationship which he enjoys with the customer.

Why Account Problems Occur

The fact that a customer is not settling his account when it is due suggests that he is short of money. Most businesses try to obtain the longest possible credit terms, especially when the interest rates on borrowed money are high. Certainly, the supplier firm must make available to its customers the normal credit facilities which are applicable to the particular industry in which it is operating. It is not, however, the function of a supplier of materials or components to act as an interest-free lending house to its customers.

When a customer exceeds the credit limit which has been agreed, the supplier must ask himself if this customer is having difficulty in meeting his commitments. The more time which elapses before payment is received, the greater the concern. Confidence in the customer's creditworthiness will decline; concern for the recovery of the money, which has been lent by means of the credit provided, will increase. A stage will be reached when the supplier company must decided that no more goods can be supplied on credit until at least part of the outstanding amount has been paid. It will put this particular customer on what is called a 'stop-list'. This means that no further dispatches may be made until at least part of the outstanding account has been cleared. If the customer still does not pay up, the supplier may decide to place the matter in the hands of his solicitors and seek to recover the debt by litigation.

No supplier wishes to take these extreme measures with a customer whose business he has hitherto valued. Before stopping deliveries, he will normally write a series of letters to his client reminding him that the account is overdue for payment. In each succeeding letter the phraseology used will become increasingly abrupt. However, providing it is done properly, personal contact in such a matter is often more effective than a letter, and there is considerable merit in arranging for the sales representative to speak to a member of the client company.

Delay in payment is not always due to the customer being short of money. In many cases it can be the result of a lack of efficiency on the part of the client's accounts department. There may be some query regarding the account and, instead of getting it sorted out, the person responsible has been dilatory.

Alternatively, the customer may be finding it difficult to obtain prompt payment from his own customers, with the result that his liquid funds are limited. He may be forced to make payment only to those of his suppliers whose products he must at all costs obtain in order to maintain his own production. For items where he has the choice of several suppliers, he can, if necessary, maintain supplies by delaying payment to one supplier and then purchasing from another should the first company put him on the 'stop-list'.

In these circumstances a supplier may need to apply only gentle pressure in order to obtain a cheque to bring the account up to date. Such gentle pressure can often be exerted best by the salesman who knows the customer personally rather than by sending a threatening letter.

Some customers can react violently to a mishandled request for an account to be settled. Some have been known to close their account with a supplier because he had the temerity to send a very standard type of reminder stating that an account was two months overdue.

One customer who received such a letter told the representative that he would buy nothing from him for three months 'to teach his company a lesson'. He paid his account immediately, and for exactly three months placed his business with another supplier. At the end of the period he resumed business, having warned the salesman not to let his accounts department send him any 'chases' in the future, because the next time it happened the account would be permanently closed.

It is, therefore, an unenviable task to have to tell a customer that his payment is overdue; still worse is to have to imply that, until a cheque is received, further deliveries against his orders may be withheld.

How to Discuss Account Problems with Customers

This is the one circumstance in which I believe that the salesman is justified in adopting what might be termed the 'us-and-them' approach. Throughout this book I have stressed the need for complete loyalty to one's own company and its personnel. However delicate the matter which you may have to handle—and account matters are among the most delicate—loyalty to your own people must remain paramount. When asking a customer to settle his account, however, it is justifiable for the salesman to position himself, metaphorically, at some distance from his accounts department and somewhat closer to his customer.

The line which the salesman should adopt is that he has a problem with regard to the next delivery of the customer's order, because his accounts department are concerned that the outstanding account is unpaid. He is, therefore, asking the customer to help him to overcome this problem by sending off a cheque. This will enable him to make sure that the delivery in question arrives on the date it is due. There should be no implication that the customer is withholding payment deliberately or is short of money, merely that this situation has been caused by some unfortunate oversight.

An approach of this kind will usually enable the customer to imply that the oversight is not his, but that of his own accounts department. He will promise to look into the matter and have it put right immediately. A cheque is then forthcoming, the customer's name is removed from the 'stop-list', and deliveries proceed smoothly

No doubt the customer will realize that the salesman has been instructed to intervene; but he will appreciate the fact that this intervention has been undertaken with the utmost courtesy and without causing needless embarrassment. The salesman will have done his duty to his company and will have demonstrated to his management that the best way of dealing with account problems in his area is to entrust him with the task of solving them.

There are, of course, cases when the gentle, courteous approach merely produces a negative result. The customer promises the salesman that he will do something about his outstanding account. But no cheque is forthcoming. The salesman is then justified in taking a firmer line. Anyone who incurs a debt is under an obligation to settle it. Having been told that his account is overdue and that this may cause future deliveries to be held up, the customer can no longer blame his staff for the delayed payment.

The salesman should remember that business is conducted for profit, and there can be no profit unless one is going to get paid for the goods or services provided. He should make it quite clear to the customer that, unless payment is received promptly, the matter will be taken out of his hands by his accounts department and further deliveries will be withheld. If there are special extenuating circumstances, he should invite the customer to explain them to him so that he may make a case to his management for credit extension.

Should this second attempt fail, the salesmen must tell the customer that, as he warned might be the case, deliveries are being withheld. If payment is still not made, he should seek the instructions of his management with regard to the future servicing of the account. He may be told to continue to make representations to the customer and to let him know that there is the risk of legal proceedings being taken against him. On the other hand, his management may decide that it is better for the salesman to withdraw completely and to instruct their solicitors to serve a writ on the customer with a view to forcing payment.

Obviously, it is very much in the interests of the salesman to try to avoid this final solution. He must do everything in his power to prevent a head-on collision between his company and his customer.

Insurance Against Further Account Problems

The best way of avoiding a recurrence of account problems with a customer is to ensure that the credit facilities which are made available to him are realistic in terms of the amount of business which you wish to maintain. If you believe that a customer is overtrading, you would be wise to see that the level of business which you transact with him does not become so great that he might become a credit risk.

There are many occasions when a customer may find it difficult to meet his commitments to his suppliers because some unfavourable turn of events has resulted in a shortage of liquid assets. This could be due to a sudden loss of business, or to the purchase of expensive new plant or premises in the expectation of increased business which has not materialized.

The good sales representative will try to find out these extenuating circumstances and to make as good a case as he can to his management for leniency, providing that some leniency is justified. He can act as 'honest broker' between his customer and his management, and many a potentially difficult account problem can be sorted out amicably by a meeting of the two parties and a frank exchange of views.

There are times when a customer, who is in temporary financial difficulty, does not explain his problem to his supplier for fear that some drastic and precipitate action may be taken to obtain payment. Equally, through lack of confidence, one's company may act forcefully and even resort to legal action against a customer, when a more understanding and tolerant approach could have prevented an ugly episode.

The role of the representative in this kind of situation can be vital. If your company's accounts people are provided with sufficient information to feel confident that the customer will win through to better times, they may be persuaded to refrain from taking punitive action. They may allow the outstanding account to remain outstanding, subject to certain guarantees, for months or, possibly, for years. Such cases do occur and usually result in the retention of the business. A customer who is well treated by a supplier over a serious financial situation will, very often, become a particularly loyal customer. He may show his gratitude long afterwards by refusing to move his business away, in spite of more attractive offers from competitive suppliers.

CHAPTER NINETEEN

PROBLEMS AND PRACTICE IN THE PURCHASING DEPARTMENT

The industrial salesman will spend the greater part of his working life in contact with the personnel of the purchasing departments of client companies. In the process of getting to know them he will establish their requirements, negotiate for their business, accept their orders and progress deliveries. He will also maintain a general servicing of their accounts, which will include the occasional investigation of service and quality complaints. From time to time he may be concerned with account difficulties; more often he will be discussing modifications to both his quality and service to accommodate and satisfy clients' changing needs.

Throughout this period of association, he will become increasingly conversant with his customers' buying methods and procedures. It is desirable, therefore, that he should have some basic understanding of the purchasing function; then he will be better able to appreciate the problems and practices of the buyers with whom he is dealing.

The Status of the Industrial Buyer

The place of the industrial buyer or purchasing officer has undergone considerable change in recent years. In the past he was usually responsible to the production manager, but increasingly the purchasing department has acquired an independent position and is often directly responsible to the board of the company. In many of the larger public companies, the purchasing officer is also a director of the company. The importance of the purchasing function has become recognized by industrial management as one of the major functions of business.

The materials and components which comprise the majority of finished products may represent over 50 per cent of the manufacturing cost. Efficient purchasing therefore becomes essential if a manufacturing concern is to make and sell products profitably in a competitive market.

The emergence of the specialist industrial buyer during the 1920s led to the foundation of the Purchasing Office Association. Among its main objectives are the maintenance of a high standard of practice in the conduct of business, increased general and technical knowledge of those responsible for purchasing, and the provision of information concerning markets, commodities and general economic conditions.

Functions of the Purchasing Department

It should be remembered that a customer's purchasing procedure is based on the manufacturing programme of his production department and that the procurement of supplies forms the first stage in the process of production. The object of efficient purchasing is therefore to have the right materials in the right place at the right time.

The purchasing function deals not only with the components and materials required for the production of the finished product. It also includes the procurement of plant and machinery, office and canteen equipment, stationery, machine lubricants and power fuels.

The main activities of a purchasing department include the following: discovery of more competitive supply sources; liaison with the design, development and production department, as well as the accounts department, to co-ordinate buying policies; maintenance of records to ensure that goods are procured in quantities and to a quality standard necessary to meet the manufacturing programme; receipt and storage of goods; issue of goods, to the production unit; disposal of scrap and waste materials which arise from the production process.

In addition to its principal function of scheduling, purchasing, receiving and storing materials, the purchasing department may sometimes be responsible for the stock-holding of finished goods and spare parts for after-sales service.

The routine work of the purchasing department includes the following sequence: receipt of requisitions from the production department for the materials and components which they require; seeking quotations; interviewing supplier's representatives and deciding the most suitable supply source, taking into account the conditions under which the goods will have to be purchased. There follows the negotiation of contracts, the raising of purchase orders and the scheduling of deliveries.

The next stage will be the follow-up or progressing of these orders to ensure that deliveries are received as specified. As soon as they are received, the goods will be checked for quantity; it is also the responsibility of the purchasing department to ensure that they are inspected and tested for quality. Finally, supplier's invoices will need to be checked and passed to the accounts department for payment.

In an industrial organization where the products to be manufactured require a complexity of materials and components, the purchasing officer must have at his disposal comprehensive records concerning supply sources and technical data. These will include a classified list of the suppliers and potential suppliers of the range of components and materials which are purchased, records of all purchases for reference purposes and records for prices and for material specifications.

An efficient purchasing department must undertake research into all aspects of the purchasing function. This will include studies of markets, taking into account price trends and seasonal variations, as well as studies of materials, cost analyses and the investigation of new sources of supply. The latter will necessitate a study of the manufacturing methods and the plant capacities of potential suppliers. There will also be periodic reviews to examine the viability of 'make or buy' alternatives: where materials or components are purchased in considerable quantity, the relative merits of buying-in or manufacturing such supplies within the company have to be considered.

A further aspect of the work of the purchasing department is the subsequent control of stocks. The purchasing officer must assess the likely requirements of the manufacturing units and maintain adequate stocks of materials and components to meet the manufacturing programme. He must ensure that records are kept of all stocks held and of goods issued to the manufacturing units. Data must be provided for the costing and budgetary control departments. Stocks must be classified and catalogued to facilitate easy identification and location both in the stores and in the production department. Finally, adequate insurance cover must be maintained for all stocks and capital equipment; in the event of damage or loss by fire or theft, the purchasing officer will be responsible to see to it that insurance claims are initiated and settled.

The control of all these activities places a heavy responsibility on the purchasing officer. He must possess the qualities of intelligence and adaptability, the ability to co-operate with others within his own organization and the respect and confidence of his suppliers.

We have spoken of the need for the salesman to acquire a professional outlook and competence. He should recognize that the modern buyer is also a man of professional status with all that that implies in terms of integrity and dedication to his work.

Many purchasing officers, and particularly those of the younger generation, are men with good educational attainment who have undergone specialized training. They bring to their work not only a considerable knowledge of purchasing principles and practice, but also of general industrial management and business economics.

The salesmen selling to industry should understand the functions of the purchasing officer and the part which he plays in co-operation with other departments within his organization. Since more than half the manufacturing cost of a product represents bought-in materials and components, it is evident that such buying-in must be on a strictly competitive basis if the product is to be made and sold competitively. Here the advice and guidance of the purchasing officer can make a vital contribution to the success of his company's operation.

Co-operation between the purchasing and the engineering departments in a large organization can often lead to standardization which reduces the number of items that have to be kept in stock and eliminates altogether a number of components of exceptional size or design.

Possible Inter-department Conflicts of Interest

The industrial salesman must be alive to the fact that the immediate interests of the purchasing and the production departments within a client company may not always be in the closest harmony. The production manager is primarily concerned with the maintenance and increase of output from his manufacturing plant. His interests will be best served if he has, at all times, an abundance of stock of materials and components which will enable him to be as flexible as he wishes in programming his production. It will assist his ease of production to be conservative in the choice of such materials and components, and he may have a marked resistance to any changes which could hazard the smooth running of his manufacturing programme.

These propensities must run counter to the best overall interests of the company. They would result in excessive and expensive stock-holding. They could cause a high wastage rate because of carelessness in the handling and use of feed-stocks within the factory. The consideration of alternative and possibly cheaper materials and alternative supply sources would tend to be limited. It follows, therefore, that a close co-operation must exist between the production and purchasing departments, based on a mutual trust and confidence.

Much harm can be done to such confidence by the irresponsible intervention of a supplier's representative, whose sole aim is to get his products considered and accepted for use within the company. It is a well understood principle in the vast majority of industrial undertakings that communication with suppliers is a function solely of the purchasing department. This need not prevent contact between the supplier and the company's design and development divisions or the production division and there is considerable mutual benefit to be derived from such liaison. Such contact should, however, always be made with the knowledge and consent of the purchasing department. Furthermore, having established such contact with the design or production personnel, the salesman should be careful to respect the interests of the purchasing personnel who must ultimately carry the responsibility for reaching all purchasing decisions. The salesman who attempts to get his product specified by the design division and his material evaluated by the production unit, thus flouting the authority of the purchasing officer, will not only damage seriously his relations with that individual but may be the cause of strained relations between the various departments within the client company.

On the other hand, the salesman who respects the interests of each department and can gain the confidence of all parties may act as a useful intermediary. On occasion his assistance in achieving reconciliation of interests can result in the acquisition or increase of business with that company.

Sometimes the salesman has to sell his products not only to the buying department but also to the production personnel. For example, he may have a grade of material which possesses all the properties of a competitive grade which is currently being used, with the added advantage that his is slightly cheaper. Because of the cost savings inherent in the purchase of his product, the purchasing department will wish to have it tested and approved by their production division. If the production personnel are satisfied, however, with the performance of the competitive material, they may be reluctant to see any changes instituted in the source of supply in case the new material creates manufacturing problems. They may either resist the request to carry out trials or be unenthusiastic about the results of the trials when they have taken place.

In these circumstances both the salesman and the purchasing department have a common interest, which is to persuade the production department to give the new material a fair trial and an unbiased assessment. The buyer may well encourage direct contact between the salesman and his production personnel because the salesman, being trained and experienced in the promotion of his product, may have greater success in overcoming their resistance and in reassuring them of the consistent quality of his product. The salesman should realize, however, that in suggesting or assenting to his personal contact with the production department the buyer will expect him to limit his discussions to matters concerning the processing of his material. The salesman should not enter into a discussion of prices or other commercial considerations with the production people, for these matters are the prerogative of the purchasing officer.

Similarly, when the industrial salesman is introducing to the market a new product, he should address himself in the first instance to the purchasing department of the client company. The buyer may decide that the new material or component has no place in his existing production requirements, but it could be of interest to the chief designer who is thinking in terms of new products to be adopted for manufacture in the following year. Therefore the buyer may arrange for the salesman to meet the design team, adding that although he does not wish to be involved in the detailed discussions he would like to be kept informed of any progress. It will be wise for the salesman to bear this request in mind. He should make a point of keeping the buyer in the picture and of advising him of the price and availability of whatever new grade of material or new component is specially developed as a result of the designer's proposals. The buyer will then have the advantage of knowing what the effect may be on the costings for the job and what delivery period he must allow in order to secure adequate supplies, if the new grade or new component is in fact adopted.

The Need for Adherence to the System

The work of the purchasing department in a large industrial organization can at times be extremely complex. Because of the multiplicity of materials and components which are purchased and which may come from many different industries, the task can only be carried out efficiently by close adherence to a clearly defined procedure.

To the uninitiated, such procedures may appear as the worst examples of excessive bureaucracy. Many salesmen tend to be impatient of the apparently cumbrous systems which operate within client companies for the requisitioning, ordering and scheduling of supplies. They despair at what may appear to be an inordinate amount of paperwork required to confirm a comparatively small purchase. But one must bear in mind the problems which would inevitably arise if any attempt were made to short-circuit the established procedure. The organization may be employing up to a hundred people solely in the procurement of perhaps a thousand different types of items within an overall purchasing budget which may run into several millions of pounds. Anything which threatens the smooth running of this complex structure is bound to be deprecated.

Centralized Purchasing

One of the features of the industrial scene over the past 20 years has been the amalgamation of companies into giant groups with manufacturing plants sited in different parts of the country. The question arises in such circumstances whether each production unit shall deal with its own purchasing or to what extent common requirements shall be met through a central purchasing department.

There are several arguments for and against a centralized purchasing system. Among the disadvantages, one must consider the problem of individual plants which are engaged in different manufacturing operations utilizing different types of processing machinery, materials and components. A locally based buyer is likely to have a more intimate knowledge and understanding of these local requirements than a centralized purchasing officer situated hundreds of miles away. In an emergency the local buyer is better placed to deal with the urgent procurement of supplies and has greater facilities for on-the-spot consultation with the production management.

On the other hand, among the advantages of central purchasing, one of the most important is that the individual production units will have several common requirements. By consolidating the individual needs of the various factories into an overall requirement, the central purchasing department has a considerably increased purchasing power for any one material or component. This obviously strengthens their negotiating position in procuring supplies. Furthermore, such a procedure can eliminate much of the duplication of effort of individual plant buyers and can minimize the wasteful duplication of paper-work. A further advantage of the central purchasing of common commodities is that the needs of one manufacturing unit may be satisfied from the surplus of another. Indeed, not only may stocks be interchanged, but purchasing know-how and accumulated experience may be pooled.

Generally speaking, in organizations where a central purchasing department has been created, it is normal for local buying departments to be retained at each of the production units. These local buyers handle the requisitioning of supplies through the central agency and the direct purchase of supplies which are peculiar to their own requirements. The salesman who has business to do with such an organization may find it necessary to sell at two locations: the local and the central buying establishments.

In negotiating for business in such circumstances one should bear in mind the differing levels of authority which may perhaps exist between the local and the central buyer. On occasion, a central buyer will recognize only those suppliers who are prepared to negotiate a group discount payable to the central buying agency on all business conducted with the individual production units. The decision to purchase will, however, remain with the local buyer who must, obviously, seek to buy as competitively as he can. Any price reduction which may be effected to secure business at the local level must, therefore, take account of the group-discount obligation that has to be incurred before locally negotiated contracts are ratified by the central buying authority.

CHAPTER TWENTY

EXPORT SELLING

To sell successfully into overseas markets the salesman requires special qualifications and a certain attitude of mind. First, he needs to understand the administrative side of export work: documentation, marine insurance, finance and all the other details of procedure necessary to sell goods abroad.

The Importance of Languages

Secondly, he should have an interest in and a liking for foreign languages. While it is true that many of those who are engaged in the export field have only a limited knowledge of the languages of the countries in which they are selling, it is obvious that before one can create any rapport with one's overseas customers one must be able to understand and speak their language with a degree of fluency.

The principles of export selling are the same as those which have been examined in considerable detail in previous chapters. It will be apparent that only very limited progress can be made in understanding a customer's motivations if one does not possess fluency of language. Colloquialisms and turns of phrase play such a large part in the conduct of negotiations that, if such things are a closed book to him, the salesman will spend much of his time with his customers floundering in an effort to understand their attitude and motives.

Coupled with this understanding of the language of the export market to which he is selling, the salesman should have an interest in and acquire a knowledge of the traditions of the people and their way of life. It is comparatively easy for the uninitiated salesman to blunder in the matter of behaviour and comment when he is dealing with customers in his own country. How much more hazardous, therefore, it is to deal in an overseas market with people whose customs and traditions differ widely from one's own.

A Liking for Travel

The aspirant to export selling should have a liking for travel. Travel in business is something very different from travelling on holiday. There is a considerable loneliness to be endured when spending weeks or months in a foreign town, especially when this temporary exile is dictated, not by choice, but by the demands of the job.

No salesman can function even adequately unless he is happy in his situation. An export salesman who dislikes the country, the food and the people among whom he has to spend a high proportion of his time will always be less than adequate. In spite of the increasing internationalism of business, it should be remembered that mankind remains parochial and the foreign salesman remains a foreigner even though he may have acquired a considerable knowledge and understanding of the language, customs and outlook of the people to whom he is selling.

Selling in the export market places greater demands on the salesman than selling in his own country. He is operating at a far greater distance from his head office than his home-based colleagues. He needs to be capable of working on his own initiative to a greater degree and for much longer periods of time. He should have a thorough technical knowledge of the product which he is selling because he does not have the facility, enjoyed by the home-based salesman, of assistance from technical service personnel at short notice.

Forward Planning and Essential Preparation

It is important that the export salesman should have a complete understanding of his company's production methods and marketing policy. He must enjoy the confidence of his management and know that his actions and decisions will carry their support. The success of negotiations with customers can be jeopardized if it is necessary for him to have to refer back to his management personnel for instructions on matters of detail. He should, therefore, try to anticipate as many as possible of the points which may arise during visits to overseas customers and to decide how to deal with them before he sets out. Such considered preparation will enable the salesman to discuss with his superiors those items which may require policy decisions.

The success of an overseas business trip is governed to a considerable extent by the care with which it has been prepared. When one has to cover long distances and visit widely scattered customers, possibly in several different countries, it is by no means easy to arrange a convenient time-table. It need hardly be said that all appointments should be confirmed in advance. A greater difficulty is to assess the amount of time one should allow for each visit. It is good advice not to be too ambitious on a foreign business trip. Business travelling can be exhausting and a tour which may last for several weeks will place a considerable strain on the salesman. He may be travelling several thousands of miles and will be living out of a suitcase all the while. He will require considerable stamina. He must also arrange his programme to ensure that he gets sufficient sleep. This can be a major problem when a tour includes night flying.

The hospitality which is likely to be extended to him by his overseas clients may be embarrassingly lavish. He must be capable of considerable self-discipline, particularly in matters of food and drink. Apart from the personal unpleasantness involved, to become unwell on a business trip can be expensive for one's company, both in the provision of medical attention and in the loss of business opportunities.

Know Your International Market

The export salesman needs to acquire a knowledge of the international industry to which his products belong. We have spoken earlier of the need to know one's competitors, their products, their policies and their motivations. In a single market, such as that of the United Kingdom, such knowledge can be acquired within a comparatively short time. When one is selling in the export field, however, one's competitors are world-wide.

In the plastics industry, for example, the leading British manufacturers of raw materials can probably be counted on the fingers of two hands. When one is selling a plastics material overseas, however, one must take account not only of all the British producers of that product, but also of those of the United States, Japan and several of the countries of Western Europe.

To keep himself informed and his information up to date, the export salesman needs to read and study the world's trade Press applicable to his particular product and the markets into which he is selling.

Export Selling is Not for the Novice

It will be seen, therefore, that export selling is not a particularly suitable field of activity for the novice salesman. It is, however, a field to which he may aspire if he has the inclination. With the very considerable world trade which is expected to exist in future years there will, undoubtedly, be good export opportunities for salesmen who have gained experience of industrial selling within their own country and a sound knowledge of their products and the applications for which they are produced.

The special qualifications necessary for success in export selling require fuller treatment than is possible within the scope of this book. Those who wish to graduate to this field of selling activity would be well advised to prepare themselves by studying, in the first place, for the Institute of Export examinations. These provide a thorough grounding in export practice and cover the general principles of commerce, marketing, geography, international trade, commercial law and export insurance.

A number of technical colleges throughout Britian will prepare students for these examinations. Alternatively, the aspirant may study for them by means of a correspondence course.

CHAPTER TWENTY-ONE

SELLING TO THE RETAILER

The motivations of the industrial buyer of raw materials or components differ greatly from those of the buyer in a retail business who purchases a product for resale in its existing form. The buyer of a departmental store or the proprietor of a small retail shop buys stock for resale. He has to decide, before he buys it, whether he can resell it. The fact that the product in question sells very well in other places does not mean that it will sell readily in his particular shop.

The Importance of 'Position' for the Retailer

Every retail business does a kind of trade which, very largely, is peculiar to itself. There are differing levels of trading which result from the area in which the shop is located and its position within that area.

Basically, there are three types of position in the retail trade. The first-class position is one that is situated in a major shopping street in which there are multiple stores to attract a steady stream of shoppers. Secondly, there are the lesser shopping streets or 'parades' which, usually, do not contain multiples and where the volume of shoppers is consequently far less. Finally, there is that peculiarly British institution the 'corner-shop', often a general provision stores, which is situated away from other retail establishments and is in a predominantly residential area.

Apart from position, area will affect the trading level of a shop. A business in a first-class position in a working-class area will carry a different type of stock to one that is in a secondary position in what is essentially a middle-class shopping area.

The art of successful retailing is to gauge accurately the level of one's market. At the extreme ends this may not be too difficult. The problem arises in the middling areas where the social level of the clientele may be very mixed. The class of clientele for which the shop has to cater governs not only the methods of retailing but also the class of goods which are stocked. Indeed, on entering a strange town, a glance into the windows of clothing and furniture shops will give one a good indication of the social level of the people who live in the area.

The Retailer Must Speculate

The retail buyer, unlike the industrial buyer, does not have a previously established outlet for what he buys. The industrial buyer knows that his factory will use so many gallons of paint or so many thousands of spools in its manufacturing programme. The buyer for a store or a shop, on the other hand, has to take a chance that whatever he buys he will be able to sell to his retail customers.

Whereas the industrial buyer has no option but to buy to satisfy the demands of his factory for raw materials or components, the retail buyer must exercise his judgment and decide whether to buy. The industrial buyer can purchase only those items which are required by his production line. The retailer is generally free to buy when and where he wishes, subject to his ability to resell the merchandise to his customers and make a profit. He can be tempted, therefore, to buy a particular line of goods by the persuasiveness of the salesman. It will be seen that in selling to the retail buyer, the personality of the salesman can be his most important asset.

If the buyer likes the salesman and is prepared to believe that a line of tea-sets or table-cloths would probably sell in his particular district, he may well be tempted to order a few 'to see how they go'. Such a situation can hardly arise in industrial selling because there are very few industrial buyers who would have either the occasion or the freedom of action to buy a few gross of a special-size washer 'to see how they go'.

The retailer is more prone than the industrial buyer to be guided by the salesman in the choice of merchandise which he should purchase. The governing factor in his buying philosophy must be the readiness with which he can resell the goods which he purchases. In seeking to form his own judgment of the suitability of a particular line of goods for his shop, he will be open to suggestion on the part of the salesman who has had experience of their suitability elsewhere.

In small retail establishments, where the buyer is personally involved in the selling operation, the choice of his purchases may be conditioned very largely by his personal belief in his ability to sell the goods. To some extent, therefore, his buying policy will be influenced by his own preferences because it is usually easier to sell something which one likes oneself. For example, the lady buyer employed by a dress-shop will be influenced considerably in her selection by dresses which she would either like to wear herself or which she would like to see worn by her customers.

The Retail Buyer's Greater Responsibility

Generally speaking, the buyer for a retail establishment, large or small, carries a greater individual responsibility within his (or her) own organization than his counterpart in industry. Whereas the industrial buyer must exercise judgment in deciding upon the source from which he will obtain his materials and components, the suitability of the goods themselves is usually established by others within his company. His technical and production colleagues will examine the specifications for the product, evaluate samples and provide a technical opinion on their acceptability.

The retail buyer, however, must not only be the judge of quality, which is something tangible; he must also assess resaleability, which is something most intangible. This assessment can be made only on the basis of knowledge and experience. The best retail buyers possess, also, a natural flair for recognizing the potentialities of a line of merchandise.

Not all retailers possess this flair. There are many who doubt their own judgment and will follow a trend rather than lead one. They will buy a line not because they believe that it will sell in their own establishment but because it is already selling in shops elsewhere.

CHAPTER TWENTY-TWO

SELLING IN THE RETAIL TRADE

So far in this book we have concentrated on selling to industry; but the same basic principles apply to all forms of salesmanship, including selling to retail customers in shops and stores. When selling in the retail sphere it is just as important to obtain the confidence of the customer and to understand his or her motivations.

The Difference between Industrial and Retail Selling

One of the most significant differences between selling to industrial customers and selling to the public is that the industrial buyer is usually experienced in purchasing the kind of materials or components which the salesman has to offer and, generally speaking, he knows what he wants. When dealing with the retail customer, however, one should recognize the fact that he (or she) may have comparatively little experience in the purchase of a particular item of merchandise and, very often, has only the vaguest idea of what he actually requires.

Selling to a commercial buyer requires the building of a connection which will result in not just one order but a sequence of transactions. We have seen that a single call seldom produces an order in industrial selling. A series of visits may be necessary to establish the customer's requirements, to arrange for the submission and testing of samples and finally to negotiate for the business, possibly on a contract basis. Over this period of visits the salesman acquires considerable insight into the motivations of his customer. He can therefore plan his selling approach in such a manner that he will create a degree of mutual trust and understanding which may form the basis of a close and continuing business relationship.

The salesman in a retail establishment, on the other hand, has practically no time at all in which to get to know his customer. They meet as strangers, yet within a matter of minutes the salesman must determine the customer's requirements and motivations and encompass all those other steps inherent in the achieving of a sale. Retail selling may therefore be regarded as a microcosm of the selling art.

Motivations of the Retail Customer

Attempts have been made to categorize shoppers so that the retail salesman, on recognizing the particular category to which a customer belongs, can respond in accordance with a set selling pattern. Since all customers are people and no two people are alike, it follows that such attempts must produce very inexact results. Nevertheless, the behaviour patterns of customers are fairly predictable in given circumstances. If we can define and recognize the circumstances which cause a customer to enter a shop, it is possible to deduce something about his probable behaviour and motivations which can be a guide in the selling process.

First, we must draw a distinction between those items of merchandise which the public buy when and where it is convenient for them to do so and those items for which they 'shop around' before reaching a decision to buy. In the category of 'convenience buying' we may place the bulk of the housewife's regular purchases of foodstuffs, cleaning materials, cigarettes, confectionery and all other sundry items in her normal household budget. The goods for which customers 'shop around' are those which are purchased less frequently, such as clothing, furnishings, and domestic appliances.

The bulk of the merchandise which comes within the convenience category is sold not by personal salesmen but by national sales promotions in the form of advertisements in the Press and on television and by window displays and interior displays in the shops. What we have to consider is the selling of goods in the second category: those for which the customer 'shops around'.

Some people only enter a shop when they have already decided on the item they intend to purchase. They may have bought the same kind of article previously or they may have been induced to make the purchase as the result of advertising or on the recommendation of a friend. One hardly needs to sell to a customer with this motive, and the salesman's function is little different from that of the assistant in the food-store or the tobacconist's. The customer's purchasing decision has been made; it merely remains to find the goods, wrap them and take the money.

The wariness which is normally apparent when a customer is undecided in his requirements will not exist in these circumstances. The salesman has, therefore, the opportunity to make a *related* sale additional to the preconceived sale which brought the customer into the shop. An obvious example of a related sale is that of accessories to the main item of purchase: a pair of gloves to go with a handbag or a tobacco pouch with a pipe.

Because the customer has entered the shop with a disposition to make his preconceived main purchase, he will be in a buying mood. He will have passed beyond the stage of having doubts about the desirability of conducting business with this particular establishment. The transition to the purchase of a related, additional article may not be difficult. This can be especially true when the preconceived purchase is of an appliance, for the salesman can bring to the customer's attention the fact that certain accessories would be either necessary or desirable. If the customer can be persuaded of this necessity or desirability, his mental attitude could be that 'I might just as well get it now rather than make a special visit to the shop at a later date'.

Equally, when the preconceived purchase is intended as a gift, the suggestion by the salesman of an accessory may be acceptable to the customer in the belief that it will increase the pleasure of the recipient. For example, a smoker will doubtless appreciate a new pipe for his birthday, but the very fact that he has a new pipe will emphasize his need for a new tobacco pouch to accompany it.

Next we come to the type of customer who has made only a partial decision with regard to his proposed purchase. He has been attracted to the notion of buying a particular item, either because he has seen it in the shop window, because it has been recommended by a friend or because he has read about it in an advertisement. Before making a final decision, however, he wishes to look at the product to assure himself of its quality and utility. Possibly he will wish to obtain further information with regard to its performance. Here the salesman can either reassure the customer and confirm his preconceived ideas, in which case he should be able to conclude the sale of the item in question or he can take the opportunity provided by the customer's interest of introducing an improved quality or a similar product in a larger size which, because of these attributes, commands a higher price. By these means he may well achieve one of the aims of the good salesman, which is to 'sell up' to obtain increased turnover and increased profit for the business.

With the majority of customers, however, there is no preconceived purchasing intention for a particular item; the customer has a need, in a very generalized form, which he hopes to satisfy. Into this category one could place the woman who is looking for a new dress to wear at a forthcoming social event or the man who is looking for a suitable gift which he might buy his wife for Christmas. In such cases the motive is to make a purchase if something suitable is found. The salesman here is required to follow the selling process through all its various stages. It is in these circumstances that the personality of the salesman and his sympathetic interest in the customer's problem may well decide whether or not a sale is achieved. A customer in this situation is seeking the assistance of the salesman; he is asking for suggestions as to a suitable type of merchandise and for guidance in his decision to make a purchase.

Finally, there is the customer whose intentions to purchase are long term. There is, for example, the bride-to-be who knows that when the times comes she will require, among a great many other things, a carpet or a washing machine or a set of saucepans. Similarly, a man contemplating his forthcoming camping holiday knows that when the time comes he will need to buy himself a rucksack or a primus stove. The immediate motive, therefore, is essentially the gathering of information with a view to narrowing the field of choice against the day when the decision to buy has ultimately to be made. The customer must be given to understand that his need can be met from the range of merchandise in stock and that the item he requires will be waiting for him when he is ready to purchase. He is then less likely to continue looking around elsewhere and possibly making his purchase from a competitor.

In these inflationary times, when the price of any particular item is likely to rise within a short period of time, the salesman stands a good chance of persuading the 'long-term' customer to make an immediate purchase in order to avoid a possible price increase. The same argument can apply more forcibly during a period of special offers and at 'Sale' time.

It must be emphasized that in considering the above categories of shopper, one is setting arbitrary limits to the customer's motivations. Human motivations vary enormously. So does the degree of susceptibility to suggestion. The good salesman will therefore use any method of classification as a basic guide only. By means of his selling technique, he will always try to amend the aims of his customers in order to steer them towards an immediate buying decision.

The Retail Selling Process

No two sales are ever identical; yet the procedure adopted in retail selling, whether it is consciously or sub-consciously applied, is similar in all instances.

Because of the variability of human nature, it is ridiculous to suggest that one can offer a blueprint for retail selling. However, certain clearly defined stages occur in the conduct of a sale, including the following:

(*a*) Reception of the customer
(*b*) Establishment of the customer's requirements
(*c*) Offer of a choice of merchandise
(*d*) Guidance towards the making of the decision to purchase
(*e*) Completion of the sale.

Let us consider as an illustration a lady buying curtain material. She is beset with a number of uncertainties. First, she is uncertain whether the store will have a quality, a colour or a pattern which will satisfy her. Secondly, she probably has only a vague idea of the price of the kind of material she would like to buy. Thirdly, because she is uncertain of her requirements, she will want to obtain some advice from the salesman. She will also be wary, because this item of purchase may loom comparatively large in her housekeeping budget. She will have some anxiety lest she may buy something which, when she gets it home, she finds she does not really like.

For his part, the salesman will need to establish certain facts. He will want to know the quality which the customer is seeking; this will depend on the price she is prepared to pay. Having established the price range, he will need to know the kind of cloth the customer is looking for, whether it is to be heavy and hard-wearing or light and delicate. He must establish whether she is looking for something plain or something patterned and also what colour she has in mind.

Before he can establish any of these things, however, there has to be some initial communication between the salesman and the customer. This begins with her reception.

(a) Reception

The manner in which the customer is received in the shop or department of the store can play a decisive part in the subsequent conduct of the sale. Like his counterpart in industrial selling, the retail salesman must control the sale. The first question which arises, therefore, is whether the salesman should approach the customer or wait until she approaches him.

Many shoppers have an instinctive dislike for the 'eager beaver' type of salesman who pounces on them the moment they cross the threshold. Any display of over-eagerness must therefore be avoided and the reception of the client should be courteous and restrained. On entering the shop or the department the customer may require a moment to accustom herself to her surroundings. More important, she may wish to take a look at the interior displays in order to gain some idea of what her requirements are likely to be.

The customer's behaviour must ultimately be the salesman's guide. If she appears to be intent on just looking around, he should be prepared to let her do so. After a while he can join her to ask if he can assist her in her selection. But if the customer enters the selling area of the shop and pauses expectantly, she is obviously asking for the salesman to attend to her requirements.

(b) Establishing the Customer's Requirements

When one is interviewing the professional buyer of an industrial company there need be no inhibitions about asking direct questions to establish his requirements regarding quality and price. In dealing with a member of the general public, however, the situation is different. The woman who is purchasing for her own consumption will certainly seek the best quality, but this will be subject to the extent of her purse. She will be very reluctant to give any indication that she has a price limit above which she simply cannot afford to buy. However, until the salesman has established in which range of price he may expect to achieve a sale, he cannot hope to engage her interest.

The customer may not wish to face too many questions at the outset, because she will not really know how to answer them, so the salesman must 'feel' his way to the information he is seeking. Having established the general nature of what is required (in this case curtain material as distinct from dress material or upholstery cloth) he should at once place before the customer something which she can look at.

In the majority of retail businesses there are three main groupings of stock from which a selection can be offered. The bulk of the stock is likely to be in a middle price range. In addition there will be a smaller stock of items of superior quality at a higher price and a cheaper range of lower-quality goods. The salesman should, initially, show the customer items drawn from his middle range in order to gauge her reactions. If this initial assessment proves to be wrong, he may move with ease either upwards or downwards. If he started with the higher-priced range the customer might think that the class of merchandise stocked was beyond the limits of her purse. Equally, if he began with the low-price end of the range, the discerning purchaser might well feel that the shop had nothing of the quality which she was seeking.

Let us suppose that at this stage the salesman produces a length of cloth which is patterned with a yellow motif on a black ground. The first reaction from the customer might well be: 'Oh, no! I don't want anything like *that*. Have you got anything in blue?'

So out may come one or two pieces in blue, of varying shades and textures. This might elicit the comment: 'I don't want anything too *silky*.'

Now the salesman can begin to ask a few questions.

'What sort of room is it for, Madam? A living room or bedroom?'

'Oh, for the living room.'

'What other colours have you in the room, Madam? Has it got to match anything?'

'The carpet is a dark blue and the suite—well, I suppose you'd call it off-white. I don't want anything too patterned.'

By now the salesman knows that the customer would possibly accept a patterned cloth, providing the design was not too obtrusive; but it is more likely that she could be persuaded towards a plain blue.

At this stage the salesman must equate his customer's requirements with the stock which he is carrying. Good stock-keeping plays an essential part in the conduct of the sale. The salesman has to be able to put his hands on those items which he wants to present quickly. A muddled stock, with merchandise scattered over the fixtures, causes delays which can distract the customer's interest and destroy the momentum of the selling process.

The customer in our example has made no mention so far of price. As he brings forward a plain blue, the salesman should therefore mention: 'This particular cloth is £3·25 a metre, Madam'.

If she does not react to the price but continues to examine the material, it is evident that she is prepared to pay in the region of £3·00 to £4·00 a metre for her curtains. However, if she appears to turn away from this particular piece of cloth and reverts back to what has previously been shown, or casts her eyes over the fixtures, the salesman should produce another length, priced at about £2·25 a metre, and offer it coupled with a statement of the price.

If £2·00 to £2·25 a metre is the price area which the customer had in mind when she entered the store, she may well indicate this by some such remark as: 'This is more the thing; but I'm not keen on that leaf design'.

This is a clear indication to the salesman that he can forget about his £3·50 to £4·00 cloths and must concentrate on a probable ceiling price of £3·00 a metre.

(c) Offer of a Choice of Merchandise

The counter is filling up with an array of materials. There is particular merit in making it apparent to the customer that the salesman is taking trouble to offer her a choice of goods. The fact that a considerable selection has been placed before her will encourage the reasonable customer to believe that she *should* be able to find something to her liking and will deter the thought that she is likely to find a better selection elsewhere. Furthermore, the fact that the salesman has taken trouble to help her makes it a little less easy for her to break off the transaction with the time-honoured escape phrase: 'Perhaps I'd better leave it for now'. There are, I know, many shoppers who are never satisfied, and every salesman has his share; but when considerable effort has been taken on their behalf the majority of people feel under an obligation to try to reach a decision.

Throughout this process of offering the customer the range of merchandise for her selection, the salesman should encourage her to handle the products. She can then assure herself that the selling points which he enumerates are genuine.

In explaining the selling features, the salesman should avoid being too technical. His special technical knowledge should be held in reserve to counter any objections which the customer may raise regarding the price or the design, the construction or the durability of the product. Unless technical information is specifically asked for, it should not be advanced: a recital of technical points may well go over the head of the customer and simply cause confusion.

Sometimes at this stage the customer, still uncertain whether to purchase, may offer an excuse as a prelude to terminating the transaction. Certain phrases, such as 'I'll have to think it over', or 'I'll talk to my husband about it', are a clear signal to the salesman that he is about to lose a sale.

To what extent should one attempt to hold a customer who is signalling that she wishes to escape? One should only do so if there is a reasonable expectation that she can, ultimately, be induced to make a purchase. While no salesman should let a sale slip through his fingers, once it is evident that he is not going to satisfy the customer he should make it easy for her to go. She is likely to leave the shop without embarrassment and with the feeling that she will always be happy to come back on another occasion because 'they do try to be helpful'.

(d) The Decision to Purchase

When it is clear that the customer intends to make a purchase but remains undecided as to which of the alternatives before her she should choose, it is up to the salesman to assist her. The fact that she has a wide selection from which to choose can be confusing. Here the salesman can help by removing those qualities, colours or designs which the customer has herself rejected. He will thus narrow the field to two or three items.

It is unwise for him to show any marked preference at this stage. Until the customer has made her final choice it may add to her uncertainty if she thinks that the salesman is advising her to buy one item when her own preference is for another.

Where a transaction involves piece-goods, it is essential to know exactly what stock is available well before the customer reaches her final decision. If she decides on the red material with the black stripes and asks for 19 metres, it will be disastrous for the salesman to find that he has only $17\frac{1}{2}$ metres of that pattern in stock. This may seem an obvious hazard to avoid; yet it does happen, particularly when one has had 'half the shop out' in an effort to satisfy an exacting customer.

If he has any doubts about the extent of his stock of any item of piece-goods, the salesman should establish the quantity the customer is likely to want before she reaches her final decision. He will then have the opportunity to steer her away from it. Once she has made her decision, that decision is likely to be final. Having made up her mind what she wants, she will be most disappointed to learn that she cannot have it; anything else which is offered to her will appear second-best. Furthermore, any feeling she may have had of obligation to make a purchase will have vanished, because it will no longer be her fault but that of the salesman. She has not wasted his time: it is he who has wasted hers.

Having reduced the area of final choice to two or three items, there is some merit in giving the customer a moment or two to make up her mind. This is particularly true when the customer is accompanied by a relative or friend and a quiet consultation is indicated. The salesman should not walk away to attend to other customers or to get on with some other work: to do so might suggest that he had lost interest in the transaction. He should say something like 'Perhaps you would like to think about it, Madam' and move down the counter, making it apparent that he is immediately available when she has reached her decision.

If, after a moment or two, she turns to the salesman and says that she still cannot decide, she is really asking him to make up her mind for her. He should then reiterate the various factors which the customer has already mentioned: the colour of the room; the colour of the carpet; the fact that the room is north-facing and she would do well to select a warm colour; or it gets a lot of sunlight and therefore she can afford to choose something cool and elegant. By taking each of these factors and applying to them the degree of suitability of the remaining choices, he can, by a process of elimination, arrive at the cloth whose texture, colour and design most closely meet her requirements.

(e) Completion of the Sale

When the customer has reached her decision to purchase, it should not be thought that the salesman's task is concluded. Nothing is more likely to give a bad impression than to appear to lose interest in the customer as soon as the money is in the till.

The customer should be treated as a guest in the establishment at all times. With an eye to her future custom, she should be treated with as much consideration and courtesy after the sale as before. The salesman should seek to commend her purchasing decision, bearing in mind that it is a not uncommon reaction to have doubts once one has bought something. If the salesman confirms the wisdom of her choice it will go a long way towards ensuring her complete satisfaction with her purchase. By sending her on her way a satisfied customer he will ensure that she will return to his shop at a later date and buy again.

The Retailer and His Merchandise

Not only does the salesman need to know and understand the motivations of his customers, he also requires a knowledge of the merchandise he has to sell. The more he knows about his products the wider will be his scope for selling them.

In an earlier chapter on industrial selling it was suggested that the salesman would make greater progress and obtain greater satisfaction from his work if the products which he handled were of interest to him personally. The same may be said of the kind of merchandise which the retail salesman is required to sell.

One's interest in one's merchandise is seldom fortuitous. To be interested in anything one needs some knowledge with which to associate it. An interest in a particular type of merchandise, therefore, must be based on knowledge of what makes it of good, bad or indifferent quality. The more that one can learn about a product the more interesting that product becomes. A man with only a superficial knowledge of his merchandise will be a superficial salesman. The greater his knowledge and interest in the products he has to sell the more successful he is likely to be.

The good salesman instinctively looks for selling points in his merchandise. The first of these will be the material which constitutes the bulk of the product: metal, wood, leather, cloth of some description, glass or ceramic, paper or plastics. Initially, one should consider the suitability of the basic material used for the product. Whereas wood or metal may be considered suitable materials for the manufacture of a tea-tray of elegant design, the non-rusting, easy-to-clean and light-weight properties of a plastics material may be more suitable for a picnic lunch-box.

Secondly, the method of construction of the product is an essential selling feature. The sewing together of the parts of fabric articles by hand or by machine, or the assembly of wooden components by glueing as distinct from jointing, will have a bearing upon the quality of the product.

The visual appearance of a product should also be considered. Surface textures can have an important appeal according to the use to which the article is to be put. Veneering or french polishing will be surface-treatment features of furniture items, as will gloss or matt finishes of radio and television sets. A well designed and well finished kitchen sink-unit will be easier to sell than one which incorporates awkward changes of profile and unsuitable materials which can collect grease and dirt and make cleaning difficult.

The performance of a product, particularly any form of appliance, will be an important selling point. A salesman retailing appliances will be expected to be able to advise his customers on all aspects of maintenance. The customer will feel reassured in making a purchase if the salesman has been able to describe authoritatively the frequency and degree of any special maintenance required. The fact that a product is easy to maintain is an obvious selling feature.

In addition to the above points, the salesman should be aware of the repute enjoyed by the products he has to sell. With an increasing number of products being nationally advertised under brand names, the salesman should recognize the importance of the manufacturer's reputation for quality and reliability and stress this in his selling message.

It will be apparent that the inside salesman, as distinct from the shop assistant serving customers with convenience items, needs to be able to express himself fluently. He should understand and be able to make the correct use of technical terms in relation to his merchandise when the occasion demands. At the same time, he should be able to convey in ordinary language the selling points which he wishes his customer to understand and appreciate. He should therefore take every opportunity to learn the meaning of technical terms and to note how those experienced in the promotion of the sale of technical and semi-technical products to the public put over their sales message in manufacturers' literature and advertisements.

Finally, the salesman must be fully conversant with the business in which he is engaged. He should know and understand the trading policy of his employers and that of the shops and stores in his locality which are in competition with them. He should make it his business to find out what is displayed in his own shop window and in the windows of his competitors. Above all, he must learn to understand the type of people for whom his shop sets out to cater. Like the industrial salesman, he must seek a harmonious relationship with them, the better to recognize and understand their attitudes and motivations.

CHAPTER TWENTY-THREE

CUSTOMER ENTERTAINING

A great deal of nonsense has become attached to the subject of business entertaining. There is a popular belief that salesmen enjoy excessively generous expense allowances which they use to bribe their customers with lunches in the best restaurants or with lavish dinner parties followed by visits to night-clubs. Like many popular beliefs, this one contains a germ of truth which has become grossly exaggerated.

There are some salesmen who use business entertaining as a form of bribery. There are some buyers who accept it as a bribe. In all walks of life there are those who will abuse and debase what are, to the majority, perfectly respectable and socially acceptable conventions. The giving and receiving of hospitality between seller and buyer is an established convention of the industrial scene and is an entirely legitimate means of promoting and furthering good business relations.

One of the main values to the salesman of customer entertaining has already been mentioned. It provides him with the opportunity of meeting his customer in a neutral setting where they can get to know one another as individuals in a relaxed and friendly atmosphere.

Throughout this book it has been emphasized that the key to successful salesmanship is an understanding of the motivations of one's customers. The majority of executives can spare little time during their normal working hours for lengthy conversation with visiting salesmen. That menace of modern life, the telephone, is a constant source of interruption. Furthermore, the environment of office or factory, the proximity of their superiors and their subordinates, can have an inhibiting effect on some buyers. Once he is away from his workaday world, however, the buyer is able to relax and to drop the barrier of reserve which may normally exist between himself and suppliers' representatives.

The legitimate use of business entertaining, therefore, is the establishment of a neutral venue for social and business contact in which more relaxed, more lengthy and more confidential discussions can take place.

The popular notion that business entertaining in general is conducted for the purpose of bribery of the buyer by the seller is illusory. Business which can be 'bought' with an occasional lunch or an evening out is plainly not worth much to the salesman. The next supplier to come along can so easily outbid him for the buyer's favour. Furthermore, any buyer who allows his purchasing policy to be influenced by the amount of entertaining which he receives from his suppliers will soon fail in his job. His successor, if he has any good sense, will not allow himself to fall into the same trap. The basic factors of acceptable quality, adequate service and competitive price are what must influence buying decisions.

Assessing the Value of Customer Entertaining

The majority of companies selling to industry encourage their representatives to do a reasonable amount of customer entertaining. The question of what is or is not reasonable must be judged by the salesman himself. The ultimate justification for the expense involved in entertaining will be based on the value to one's company of the outcome, in terms of the maintenance or increase of business.

In reaching the decision to entertain a customer, one should have some clearly defined purpose. Very often a salesman will invite a customer to join him for lunch largely out of habit. If a customer's business is such that some regular entertaining appears to be justified, one need not condemn the salesman for continuing a habit which, over months and possibly years, has contributed to a close and friendly relationship. He should, however, recognize and establish a motive for such entertaining; the very action of doing so will ensure that he makes proper use of the opportunity it provides to further his commercial aims with that customer.

Apart from getting to know his customer and providing the opportunity for the customer to get to know him, the salesman can use the occasion of a business lunch or dinner to seek information or to discuss matters which, because of their intricacy, cannot be discussed adequately during a visit to the customer's office. Price negotiations, for example, are sometimes difficult to conduct with a buyer who is being interrupted constantly by the telephone on his desk. The salesman will require his undivided attention in order to bring such a matter to a satisfactory conclusion.

In the relaxed atmosphere of a bar or a restaurant, the salesman may learn from his customer useful information concerning the client company's processes and trading activities in the market generally. Such information may not necessarily be confidential but it can contribute to a better understanding of the customer's problems.

It has become increasingly evident in recent years that many industrial organizations encourage their purchasing and technical staff not only to accept hospitality from supplier companies, but also to reciprocate. This enlightened attitude towards business entertaining underlines the value which this form of supplier/customer liaison has for both parties. Client firms recognize the need for rapport with their suppliers and appreciate the benefits which accrue when the personnel of a supplier company understand their general trading philosophy. A good supplier/

customer relationship depends on mutual trust which, as I have said before, has its foundation in mutual respect and understanding between the individuals concerned. A moderate amount of reciprocated hospitality can help to foster such goodwill.

How to Conduct Business Entertaining

Apart from the expense involved, customer entertaining is time-consuming. However, provided that one is discerning in the choice of customer and some thought has been given to the use to which the opportunity is to be put, the time spent with a customer at lunch or in the evening can be more productive than several conventional calls made at his office during working hours.

The good salesman uses any and every opportunity to sell to his customer. This does not mean that he should 'talk shop' all the time or even most of the time. He should use these semi-social occasions to sell himself and to sell his company. The more intelligent the salesman, the more subtle will be this selling of his own personality and the promotion of the desired image of his company. He will seek to implant in his customer's mind the impression that he is not only a pleasant and reasonable individual but also a dependable and a reasonable man of business. Similarly, he will seek to impress upon his customer that the company which he represents is reputable in its dealings and reliable in its undertakings.

It follows that when entertaining a customer the salesman will select a venue which is appropriate to the occasion. While it is fairly obvious that one would not select a second-rate establishment in which to entertain a customer, over-lavish hospitality can, on occasion, prove to be self-defeating.

When selling to industry one meets all types of people. The level of entertaining which may appeal to one customer may not appeal to another. The sophisticated type of establishment where one might entertain a senior executive of a large industrial firm could be an entirely inappropriate setting in which to have a quiet meal with the under-buyer or the assistant production controller. There are many people who occupy responsible positions in industry who have neither the aptitude nor, indeed, the desire for the 'sophisticated' life. They will feel much more at home in a pleasant but unpretentious pub than a five-star restaurant and will talk more readily over a pint of bitter than a gin and tonic.

The best policy, therefore, is to invite the customer to select the venue. Local people usually know their local eating and drinking establishments and often prefer to be entertained by their suppliers in surroundings which are familiar to them. When one is entertaining personnel from large firms, it is worth bearing in mind that sometimes there is an unwritten rule within the company that certain local hostelries are 'reserved' for the use of senior executives only. Those who occupy more lowly status are expected to confine themselves to less exalted establishments. It will, therefore, save any embarrassment if you seek the guidance of your guest before you make a table reservation.

Conviviality and Conversation

In the modern industrial and commercial world, heavy drinking has ceased to be an essential qualification for successful salesmanship. The penalties which attach to drinking and driving in Britain preclude the travelling salesman from exceeding the legal limit of consumption of alcohol. This is generally well understood by customers, who have no wish to encourage a salesman to break the law and risk losing his livelihood. Those customers who enjoy a few drinks are best entertained in the evening, when one's car is safely locked up for the night in the hotel garage. No salesman need drink excessively if he does not want to. Moderate imbibing, however, is conventionally part of the giving and receiving of hospitality, and the man who never drinks sets himself somewhat apart from his fellows. The point need not be laboured. It is sufficient to say that one needs to be an exceptionally brilliant salesman to compensate for being a teetotaller.

When playing host, either to a single customer or to a party of customers, it is essential to put your guests at their ease and to get them talking. This is the way to get to know them as people as distinct from buyers, works managers or what-have-you. In order to create understanding and goodwill, especially on these semi-social occasions, the salesman needs to be interested in other people's interests. Please note that I do not say that he must have a lot of interests himself. He does not need to be a footballer to have an interest in football. He does not even have to have an interest, personally, in football; but he should be capable of showing an interest in other people's interest in football.

The salesman should try to learn as much as possible about the leisure interests of his customers, not so much to be able to talk about them but to be able to inquire about them. It is not necessary to be knowledgeable on such subjects. People like to talk. They like to talk about the things they know and which interest them. If you can get a man on to a subject which is his 'hobby-horse' he will divulge his innerself to you more readily than if you confine the conversation to only those subjects which interest you. There are times, indeed, when such conversations can become somewhat fatiguing for the salesman. He should remember, however, that he is a professional and that it is a very important part of his job to know truly and understand those to whom he is required to sell.

CHAPTER TWENTY-FOUR

THE FIELD SALES MANAGER

In previous chapters I have tried to show that selling can be an intrinsically rewarding career. Many who begin selling in their twenties are content to remain salesmen all their working lives. Every selling assignment offers a new challenge, and the skills one acquires over the years are re-tested constantly by changes in customers' needs and new marketing techniques. For those who seek wider responsibilities, however, a first step is promotion to field sales manager.

This branch of management is so closely linked to selling that it has a place at the conclusion of this book.

A Necessary Transformation

When you become field sales manager you should realize that your primary task is to control the activities of the salesmen reporting to you. You must train them, inspire them, lead them as captain of a team. It will be important that you have 'gone through the mill' as a salesman yourself. Only if they know you have done the job and done it with above average results are they likely to give you their full confidence.

This may seem pretty obvious, but the point is that it is often extremely difficult for the successful salesman to make the transition to successful manager. You will do so only if you accept that you have changed your function. You are no longer required, primarily, to sell. Indeed, you may have to resist a very natural desire to go on selling.

Managers get their results through other people. In your case, sales results have to be obtained through your salesmen. This means taking a step back and letting them get on with the job of selling to your company's customers. *Your* job is to control their activities, not to do their work for them.

Two Essential Qualities

Like any other manager, as field sales manager you have to achieve results through other people; but unlike most managers, your subordinates—your salesmen—are geographically spread. Also, they are exposed constantly to attrition by the customers on whom they are calling. For these reasons a high proportion of your time will have to be spent providing them with leadership and training. Leadership is an essential support for salesmen working single-handed on territories away from company headquarters and physically cut off from their colleagues. Training is necessary to combat the wearing down process which can result from constant customer contact.

There are many other important aspects of field sales management such as forecasting, target-setting and organization. But the vital ones are leadership and the ability to train people. These require qualities which are not necessarily present in the successful salesman, and it is for this reason that the exceptionally good salesman does not necessarily make an exceptionally good manager.

Field Sales Management Functions

Apart from the obvious hazard of cramping the style of your salesmen, if you attempt to maintain a selling role you are likely to neglect those functions of management to which you should be devoting full attention. You have a full-scale management job to perform. You should understand fully the company's policies and procedures and be able to interpret these to your salesmen. You should know the objectives of the company in terms of desired sales volume and market penetration. You should set targets for your salesmen in terms of the sales you expect them to achieve within agreed periods of time and you should devise methods to check and control progress. You must check the movements of your salesmen to make sure that they are deployed in the most effective manner. You must ensure that selling efforts are balanced between the various products in the range and that the sales policy of the company—particularly with regard to price and settlement terms—is adhered to. You must watch customers' credit standing and make appropriate recommendations to Head Office when necessary. But, above all, you must champion the men under your command and the efforts they are making to gain and maintain business. You must try to resolve any problems they are having regarding service or product quality and seek to remove all unnecessary obstacles which prevent them from getting full satisfaction for their customers.

Beyond this, you have one more vital task: the motivation of your salesmen. Fanciful as it may sound, you have to keep 'the men at the front' inspired, and this is the most demanding aspect of your job.

Setting Objectives

The broad objectives you will have to set for your salesmen will be indicated by the general objectives of the company: to achieve a certain volume of sales in a given area of the market at a given return over a given period in a given range of materials or components. As field sales manager it is your job to take these requirements and convert them into realizable sales objectives for each of your salesmen.

Once you know the overall objective, you have to work out how you are going to achieve it. The first thing to do is to decide how much of the required business is likely to be contributed by existing customers on the various territories. Obviously, this business must be safeguarded. Customer satisfaction with regard to quality, service and price has to be checked regularly, and you will need to instruct your area salesmen as to the appropriate percentage of their time they should devote to looking after this existing business.

Once you have decided how much of your human resources, in terms of your salesmen's time and energies, are to be devoted to protecting what you already have, you must now consider what steps to take to obtain the necessary additional business which will be needed to reach your targets. This entails sitting down with each salesman in turn and trying to identify the potential business available on his territory.

You may decide that some of this business is so firmly held by competitors as to be practically unassailable in the short term. There may be other pieces of business which will require tailor-made products or very special servicing (such as deliveries twice a week to a location off the beaten track) which would make it uneconomic. There may be business offered where the technical requirements of the product needed cannot be met—or could be met only with difficulty by your factory. The retention of such business would always be difficult, might be a serious drain on your factory's output efficiency, and could demand a disproportionate amount of the salesman's time to service.

Some items of business available to your salesmen may, on the face of it, seem attractive by promising long production runs at good prices. The snag could be that the firms concerned are of an uncertain credit-worthiness. You will have to ask yourself whether you are likely to be able to get the amount of credit needed to support the business. If not, or if deliveries get held up by your company due to difficulty in getting the customers concerned to pay their accounts when due, a lot of selling effort will have been wasted.

In each of the above cases you would need to ask yourself if your salesmen would not be better employed in the pursuit of more rewarding business.

You are very likely to find yourself frequently at variance with your salesmen on the question of what is or is not a worthwhile business prospect. Of course, you should listen carefully to the case a salesman makes, and if he holds strong views about the potential value of certain pieces of business it may be advisable to make a joint visit to the customer concerned to verify the facts. But it is important that you should be on your guard and not be talked into supporting efforts to negotiate for new business on uncertain information. As we have seen, the acquisition of new business can involve one's company in consider-able expenditure in the form of product modification, the manufacture of special samples or protracted technical discussions. If there is a reasonable chance that, all things being equal, your salesman will end up getting a sizeable contract on good terms, then all this effort and expense will have been justified. But an over-enthusiastic salesman having misread the true facts of the case, can involve your company in a great deal of misapplied effort which may come to nothing.

Bearing in mind that your most important resources are the skills and energy of your salesmen, you have a special responsibility to ensure that these are utilized effectively and are not frittered away chasing what may turn out to be unrewarding business.

Organizing Your Resources

Once you have identified the additional business the company needs and pin-pointed where you hope to obtain it, your next step must be to devise the means of getting it. You will need to organize all the resources available to you. Beginning with the salesmen themselves, you will need to agree the number and frequency of their calls on the prospective customers. But this is only a beginning. Sales literature, price lists, samples have a part to play in the drive for new business and need to be prepared. Technical staff must be alerted on the technical requirements of the potential customers in question, their recommendations acquired and transmitted to the salesmen.

This organization of resources to back up the work of the salesmen is a vital part of field sales management. It is something that the salesman cannot do for himself. It would be an undesirable distraction from his primary role of selling. It is also a task which often requires for its execution a degree of authority within the company not usually held by the area salesman. It is, indeed, essentially a management function requiring fine judgement. You must try to balance the cost to the company of providing the necessary resources to gain new business against the ultimate value to the company of the business once you have got it.

Having decided your objectives and planned the use of the resources at your disposal, your next task is to ensure that all concerned—and especially your salesmen—are aware of what you hope to achieve and are motivated to play their part to the full.

How to Motivate Your Salesmen

We have seen in earlier chapters some of the problems with which, day after day, week after week, the area salesman has to cope. How do you motivate him?

The salesman works alone. He is detached from the ordered discipline of life in the office or the factory. If he is to do his job well he must exert a high degree of self-discipline throughout his working hours. He must sustain his effort in spite of adverse weather, when travelling conditions are difficult or worse, when his clients are tiresome, ill-tempered or down-right objectionable, when things go wrong and he is blamed for broken delivery promises or product failure. In spite of all these inherent difficulties of his job, the field salesman is expected to maintain his enthusiasm and a determination to win business.

In the selling of consumer goods, payment of commission to salesmen is considered one of the best motivators and is widely practised. But in the industrial sector the commission system poses many problems. Much of industrial marketing tends to be selective. Customer needs vary enormously and, as we have seen, the field sales manager must weigh the advantage of certain pieces of business against production capacity and capability and the company's overall marketing plans. A salesman with the authority to conduct price negotiations faces the obvious danger of accepting low-price business to create turnover which will earn him a commission. Such business may prove, subsequently, to be totally uneconomic, particularly if it entails special manufacture at high production cost.

There is the further problem of the movement of large user accounts from one sales area to another, and the unfairness which results when one salesman's commission drops through no fault of his own, whereas that of another increases fortuitously.

The payment of commission to industrial salesmen often creates difficulties with other staff. Technical personnel, as well as sales office staff, frequently consider with justification that important pieces of business are gained and held by a team effort in which their own contribution has been not less than that of the commission-earning salesman.

That the use of the commission system for the motivation of industrial salesmen is invalid has been proved by the very large number of industrial product firms who have abandoned its use. The general pattern today is for such companies to pay their salesmen a flat rate for the job, thus providing financial security for the man and his family regardless of the fluctuating pattern of his sales.

Self-Esteem as a Motivator

If we exclude monetary incentive, how does one motivate the man who is selling to industry?

Experience has shown that there is an alternative motivator to money. It is a sense of personal achievement. The opportunity for self-realization certainly exists for the industrial salesman. Whether or not he can achieve it depends very largely upon the attitude of mind of his sales manager.

There are few forms of commercial activity which provide as much scope for the realization of personal achievement as selling. The excitement produced by the challenge of a worthwhile piece of potential business is surpassed only by the personal satisfaction to be gained by winning it. Few salesmen ever become oblivious to the pleasure of getting an order!

But the job satisfaction of the salesman must lie in his belief that his efforts are of value to his company. He must know that his success is recognized and appreciated. His self-esteem is a vitally important asset for his company. Its maintenance, by means of a high standard of performance, is his strongest motivation.

A salesman's satisfaction in his work can, however, be destroyed easily by inept managerial practices. It is a strange fact that a salesman's keenness for his work is seldom undermined by all the apparent problems inherent to his job, such as the difficulty of obtaining business, the need to handle difficult customers and the multitude of hazards imposed by modern traffic conditions and an unpredictable climate. This is, surely, because each of these difficulties presents a challenge to his professional skill. What can demoralize him, however, are those circumstances which are beyond his ability to handle, circumstances which destroy the very assurance and esteem upon which his personal effectiveness must depend.

The greatest of these is an apparent lack of trust on the part of his manager. The good salesman has a strong personal involvement in his territory. The customers he serves are *his* customers, their care *his* responsibility. This is why it is so important that he should be included in all negotiations with the accounts on his territory, even though, for valid reasons of company policy, there may be occasions when you, as his sales manager, or more senior personnel, must intervene. Because these customers belong to him, the salesman believes that his opinion and advice should be considered before policy decisions which affect his clients are implemented. One of the surest ways in which a manager can kill a salesman's interest in his job is to appear to by-pass him and deal directly with his customers.

It is equally important that the salesman in the field should not feel that he is forgotten by his manager. A man who is working some far-flung provincial territory can easily imagine himself an outcast whose hopes and fears are completely disregarded by the people at Head Office. It is a vital aspect of the sales manager's task to care for his field salesmen and to be as attentive and concerned about their problems and complaints as he would be about those of one of his most important clients. Indeed, the attitude of mind of an area salesman responsible for a large number of customers may have repercussions no less important to the company's future trading fortunes than the attitude of the buyer of a single large-user account.

A highly motivated salesman is therefore likely to be one whose manager has a keen appreciation of human behaviour. I am not suggesting, however, that you should attempt to mollycoddle your salesmen. On the contrary, if the selling task is to remain a challenge, targets must be set which stretch the salesman. If the cliff face to the summit of success is too easy to climb the challenge will not exist. But in asking a man to set his sights on a difficult target, make sure that the demand you are making is not so impossible that he is bound to fail. To do so would be to destroy his self-esteem. The salesman needs the elixir of repeated success to motivate him, and the targets which are set should be obtainable.

Providing you have selected the right calibre of individual at the outset, the subsequent motivation of your field salesmen should be a combination of high expectation and positive assistance. A man of intelligence and integrity will maintain a continuous effort providing he believes that his manager is working for him and not against him. Not only should his successes be acknowledged but his failures, too, should be recognized. This is because the conscientious salesman is as much affected by his failure to secure a sale as by his success in winning it. When things are not going well for him the man in the field has an even greater need for his manager's interest and concern. In industrial selling, failure to gain or retain business may not be solely the fault of the salesman. It may not be his fault at all. There may be short-comings in the support the man has been given. Providing the manager's concern about his apparent failure is positive he will be encouraged to keep trying until ultimate success is achieved.

On taking control of a sales force you should always bear in mind the fact that there are bound to be weaknesses in every salesman. Your first approach should be to try to help him overcome them. What is profoundly more important, however, is that every good salesman is likely to have certain specific attributes, the greatest of which will be his overriding need for personal achievement. The best help you can offer is your assistance and encouragement in bad times as well as good. This will create the confidence and self-esteem which will drive him on towards success.

The Salesman's Selling Performance

As field sales manager your task is to see to it that all the salesmen in the team are working effectively and efficiently. This means helping them to capitalize on their individual strengths and, where possible, to overcome their individual weaknesses.

The first step is to examine each man's selling performance to find out just what his strengths and weaknesses are. The only way to do this is to join him on his territory and make a series of calls with him. You will want to find out how he approaches his customers, the way he responds to their queries, how he presents the selling features of his products and the way he reacts to customers' objections. Before you rush to do this, however, it is as well to pause for a moment and to consider the salesman's possible reactions to *you*.

He will realize that you are about to put him under the microscope, so to speak, and few people like having their boss peering over their shoulder. I suggest you should be candid. Tell him that you want to get a first-hand impression of the business he is handling and the potential on the territory. Say you want to see for yourself the kind of problems he has with existing and potential customers and to find out how he is dealing with them. Although he may not welcome the idea of being 'inspected', he will know where he stands with you. Any initial hostility on his part is likely soon to evaporate once he realizes that you are out to help him do a better job and are not merely trying to pick holes in his salesmanship.

You may find that some of the team of salesmen under your control vary considerably in age, experience and their years of service with the company. Some may be young and full of enthusiasm but lacking experience. These men are likely to respond very favourably to your arrival on their territories, because they will recognize their inexperience and will be anxious to learn anything you can tell them. Others, however, could be in their forties or fifties and may consider that they have forgotten more about their jobs than you are ever likely to be able to teach them. Each man will have to be treated differently if you are to get the most out of him in co-operation and performance.

Bearing in mind the motivational importance of the salesman's self-esteem, you should always be on your guard to avoid saying or doing anything which might deflate his ego. But you can enhance his self-esteem and add considerably to his motivation by encouraging an increased pride in his work.

Begin by getting your salesmen to take pride in the achievements of the company. It matters little whether the firm is large or small. What does matter is that it is successful. What matters is that it competes with its rivals and does so at a profit. There is no harm in a little basking in reflected glory, and to know that he represents a firm that is successful and respected gets a salesman off to a good start.

Secondly, make sure each salesman realizes the importance of his role in the company's continuing success. It is a sobering thought that the prosperity of a business depends very largely on the volume of its sales, and that the volume in turn depends, very largely, on the effectiveness of its salesmen. They must achieve consistently good results in terms of orders to keep the machines running at optimum production levels to ensure both an adequate return on capital for the shareholders and job security for all those employed in the company.

Thirdly, it is important to the salesmen's self-esteem that they should know what is going on within the firm. Because they are working on their own for most of their time, the more information you can share with them, the more involved they will feel in the company's current activities and future fortunes.

Field Sales Training

Your examination of the salesman's selling performance begins before you actually arrive at the customer's premises. You will want to know the state of play with this particular account. When was the last call made? What products does the customer use, and from whom is he currently buying? Which of the company's products were introduced on the last call? What objections, if any, did the customer raise? Was an order obtained? If not, what were the customer's reasons for refusing to buy?

A conversation on these lines should quickly establish the extent to which the salesman has become involved with this particular customer. You will soon perceive whether he is optimistic or pessimistic about his chances of gaining business here in the near future and the possible lines of approach which may be needed to improve the situation.

The next question is what the salesman considers is the aim of the proposed visit. Remember what I said in Chapter Five about defining objectives. If he is prepared to call on a customer in the spirit in which one might decide to climb a mountain—'because it is there'—you will have detected a serious flaw in his attitude to his job!

This implied woolly-mindedness is not as rare as one might suppose. Salesmen covering the same territory year in, year out, are liable to lose objectiveness. A customer is visited because he has always been visited. The fact that the nature of his business—or, indeed, the nature of *your* business—may have changed during recent years, may not have registered sufficiently in the salesman's mind.

'I've always called on old Henry whenever I've made this trip. No, he doesn't take much from us these days, but he's an old friend and I like to keep in touch.'

Think for a moment of the cost to your company of keeping this salesman on the road and couple that thought with your need to achieve certain objectives in terms of turnover and profitability. Can you afford to have your limited resources expended in this manner? Once you have met 'Old Henry' and have decided just how much—or how little—business your company is likely to get from him this year, next year and the year after, you will be able to answer that question.

This preparatory discussion with the salesman will tell you much you did not previously know about the customers you are proposing to visit. It will also tell you much you did not previously know about the salesman and the way he thinks.

When you make a joint visit to a customer with one of your salesmen with the object of assessing his selling performance it is obvious that he must take control of the interview. Unless he does, the whole purpose of the call is destroyed. But there are problems. Firstly, the customer will expect you, as the senior man, to take charge of the proceedings. He will think it odd, to say the least, if you appear content to let your subordinate take the lead. In some sales organizations, particularly those supplying consumer goods to the retail trade, the manager is advised to tell the customer, at the outset, that the call is being made for training purposes. I doubt, however, if this approach would be received very happily by a buyer in the industrial sector. Not only might he consider his time was being wasted, but his reactions to the subsequent sales presentation would almost certainly be self-conscious and artificial. As for the hapless salesman, any self-esteem he might have possessed would surely be in tatters before the interview was over.

A better way is for the sales manager to have a particular matter he wants to discuss with the customer. This may be about the provision of special discount terms or some similar subject which logically might require a management decision and be outside the area salesman's normal terms of reference. This is, if you like, the manager's 'cover story', providing him with a plausible reason for his presence. This little deception will do no one any harm and will save considerable mbarrassment. Once he has concluded his discussion with the customer on this specific issue, the manager can henceforth take a back seat, letting the salesman proceed with his sales presentation.

After the call is over and you have left the customer's premises you should make a point of discussing the visit with the salesman. This is your opportunity to implement the training aspect of your role of sales manager.

Your aim must be to identify the weaknesses in his selling performance and to show him how improvements can be made. But the last thing you can afford to do is to deflate him. Remember always the importance of his self-esteem, his confidence and his enthusiasm for his job. These assets are so difficult to foster yet can be destroyed in a moment with ill-considered criticism.

The first thing to bear in mind is that the salesman will have been influenced throughout the interview by your presence. The manner in which he has handled the conversation with the customer might well have been different had you not been there. According to his temperament he may have over- or under-projected his personality. Since he was conscious of the fact that you were listening to his every intonation, watching his every move, it would hardly be surprising if his performance appeared stilted or forced. Make due allowances and bolster his flagging self-confidence by commending him for those aspects of the interview which you think he managed rather well.

The next step is to try to expose his shortcomings. Do not tell him where you think he went wrong because his instinctive reaction will be to defend his mistakes. The better way is to ask him questions. Find out *why* he reacted in the way he did to the customer's questions about the product; *what* was his reason for explaining the selling features of the product in the way he did; *how* did he expect the customer to respond to this kind of approach?

This type of interrogation, avoiding the use of leading questions, should enable the salesman to begin to see *for himself* where his weaknesses lie. Only if your questions fail to achieve this result should you need to *tell* him what his faults are.

You may think that the stress I have placed on the need to avoid direct criticism of the salesman is a bit excessive. But in dealing with men who spend their working lives constantly in contact with customers one must never forget how vitally important is their confidence in their own talents and skills. These may not be as developed as you would wish, but they are the foundations on which you have to build. Unless a man *thinks* he knows how to sell and *believes* he can be successful, all the advice and training in the world will be to no avail.

On this question of field sales training there is one final point that should be made. Throughout this book I have tried to emphasize the importance of self-discipline in successful salesmanship.

The salesman works without the supervision normally present in office or factory. He does not clock on or clock off. He is largely his own master. He decides the hour he will start in the morning and the time of night he will return home. He writes his reports whenever and wherever he chooses. His sales manager visits his territory intermittently, and for much of the time his personal appearance, the condition of his car and the samples he carries are free from scrutiny. He has great freedom, and for some men at some times such freedom can become a burden. Even the best motivated salesmen wilt occasionally under the stress of modern travelling and the strain of constant customer contact. They need your help to support this burden.

The best help you can give is to set standards of performance and insist they are maintained. These will vary according to the trade or industry, the product or the service with which your company is concerned. In general, however, you should set standards for all the main activities that the salesman is required to perform. Many of these we have already discussed at length. They will form part of the recurrent field training which you undertake during your territorial visits. But there are other performance standards which should be part of each man's routine.

Establish the number of calls you expect him to make per day, per week or per month. Subdivide these into calls on existing accounts and prospective accounts. Instruct him to send you a regular report on his movements. Not only will this tell you how he is spending his time; it is valuable discipline for him. Promptness in submitting reports should be insisted upon. Again, this keeps the man up to the mark, compels him to resist the temptation to 'leave it over till tomorrow'. Have him ring the office daily to confirm his itinerary. Periodically, check his call reports. If the standards set are not being adhered to, ask for an explanation.

Work out, in consultation with each salesman, targets of business to be obtained, and at agreed intervals check the results achieved against the target. Variances will require explanation and will compel the man constantly to analyse his progress.

By insisting upon these simple disciplines you will help your salesmen maintain self-discipline, motivation and the sense of satisfaction that comes when a good job is well done.

CHAPTER TWENTY-FIVE

SELLING IS COMMUNICATION

Effective selling requires effective communication. The salesman's use of words is his stock-in-trade.

Communication is not simply a matter of talking. We all know the man with 'the gift of the gab'. He buttonholes us on the slightest pretext. He pours one anecdote after another into our unwilling ear, confident we are as interested as he in his manifold experiences. He is oblivious of our glazed look, our desperate desire to escape.

Noises emitting from the face are not communication. Listen to a gathering in a pub or at a party. The hubbub may be deafening but is anyone really saying anything worth listening to? What may be acceptable as so-called social conversation will seldom suffice for effective communication in business.

When a salesman converses his purpose is to sell. He should seek to generate a sufficient understanding of the merits of his product to persuade his client to buy. Remember that the response of the person to whom you are speaking is as vital as the words you use to express yourself. And the quality of that response will depend on several factors.

First, try to detect your client's state of mind. Is he really in an attentive, responsive mood? Or has he got a problem on his mind, something he has set aside for a moment while he listens to what you have to say but which he knows he must attend to urgently the moment the interview is over? Maybe it is a machine breakdown that is holding up production. Or a threatened dispute on the shop floor needing his intervention. Or an unwelcome meeting with his managing director to review last month's low output figures! Whatever it is, while he has something like this nagging at the back of his mind he is unlikely to be able to give you his full attention.

The environment in which the conversation occurs may have a marked effect upon the quality of the listener's attention. The factory manager strolling with you through the assembly shop may *appear* interested in the merits of your materials handling equipment. But half of what you are saying could be going in one ear and out the other if he has spotted some badly stacked boxes that could be a safety hazard. While he mentally notes to have a word about it to his foreman later, he has lost track of your pursuasive arguments.

Your client's attitude is also important. If he has a prejudice against

171

your company or its products, based on hearsay or some unfortunate past experience, do not imagine that he will be swayed easily by your well-reasoned arguments alone. If his poor opinion of your firm is based purely on fact, it could be true that he will revise his opinion if you can prove to him that the situation has been corrected. But many of us base our opinions not on facts but on our attitudes. An attitude is a *pre-disposition* to form certain opinions. It is often a background of feeling, a reaction to what we *believe* to be the case rather than what we *know* to be the case.

Let us say that a customer bought goods from your firm several years ago and suffered losses because they were of inferior quality. He may have vowed never to make that mistake again. Despite the fact that the quality of your products may now be vastly improved and is highly regarded by other users, your client may persist in his poor opinion of your merchandise. It will be an opinion based, not on reason, but on his emotive experience. It is a sad fact that many people use their reason, not to get at the truth of a situation, but to defend their attitudes.

To achieve effective communication, one needs to take account of these factors. If the client is failing to concentrate because of conflicting thoughts, it may be as well to postpone your discussion to a more opportune occasion. If the venue offers distractions, avoid presenting arguments that require undivided attention. And when you are faced with a customer whose attitude is antagonistic, recognise that you must first change this attitude before you can hope that he will be receptive to logical argument.

Do not overlook the barrier to effective communication that exists between well-meaning people when they have different backgrounds and cultures. As our society becomes increasingly multi-racial, the salesman needs to take account of this factor. Colour and creed aside, there are differences in outlook between North and South in Britain and sometimes even between one county and another. When strangers first meet to talk business, therefore, it is often helpful to open the discussion with a topic that is familiar to both. A matter of common interest can quickly put two people on an equal footing, removing tension and creating favourable attitudes.

Consideration for others plays a large part in good conversation. When talking with clients it is worth remembering that the other person may be just as anxious as you to express himself. He may want to contribute his ideas and opinions as well as hearing yours. To set off on a rambling discourse without regard to the reactions of your listener may well get you dubbed a bore. Beware the tell-tale signs of wandering interest. Watch his facial expressions and monitor the level of his interest in what you are saying. Most of us betray our inner thoughts by an involuntary creasing of the brows when something is said that jars; or by the quick smile that indicates our sympathy with a particular point of view.

Remember, too, how important it is to let the other person interject. He may want to clarify a point you have made or correct a mistaken impression you may have formed. Few things are more vexing than wanting to make an observation and finding oneself prevented from getting a word in edgeways! How often have we all suffered from the talker who will not cease his tirade and who raises an admonishing finger, snapping: 'Just a moment. Let me finish!' How we wish he would!

Logical Argument

The ability to argue logically is a powerful sales aid. We can all argue, of course—particularly if we feel strongly about something. There are some people who seem to spend their lives arguing, determined to have the last word. But the salesman's purpose is not to have the last word. It is to get the order. He is not out to antagonize his client but to win him over. This can be done only by persuasion. The extent to which it is advisable to argue with a customer is something the salesman must decide according to the circumstances. But if he does decide to argue his case he should do so competently. He should know something of the techniques which contribute to sound and successful argument. If he knows what these are and how they should be used, he is likely to win rather more arguments than he will lose.

In any argument, the burden of proof lies with the person who has made the assertion. If one's client listens to a recital of the significant factors of the product or service he is being offered and then declares that he cannot place an order, one is entitled to ask why. (In his turn, the client can show one the door, if he feels so inclined!) But in any serious business negotiation it is customary for the buyer at least to attempt to justify to the seller his refusal of an offer. If the buyer asserts his reasons for refusing to place business and the salesman—however politely—challenges those reasons, the burden of proof lies with the buyer.

To break down the client's contention, to persuade him that his view is incorrect, to encourage him to change his mind, counter-arguments must be advanced to show him that he has either incorrect evidence or insufficient evidence to prove his case. This is not always an easy thing to do. As a first step, it is necessary to decide what kind of argument the customer has put up.

Let us suppose that he has told the salesman that he will not buy from him because he will only do business with manufacturers and the salesman's firm are merely factors. 'I know that in this trade factors get their supplies from all sorts of sources. I speak from experience when I say that if I buy from a factor I will not get a consistent product. I will be buying trouble.'

Now this kind of argument is what is called *argument by induction*. The client is basing his assertion on his observation of certain facts—namely, that in his particular trade factors apparently obtain the goods they resell from miscellaneous sources and that factors supply an inconsistent product. From his observations he has drawn a general law: that *all* factors, because they *all* buy from a variety of sources, *all* supply an inconsistent product.

There are three main methods by which one may attack an inductive argument. The first is *to question whether sufficient examples have been examined to justify the assertion which has been made.* In this instance, is the customer basing his case on too limited a knowledge of the trade?

Secondly, one must question *whether the examples cited are sufficiently representative.* Are the firms of factors the customer is talking about operating in a manner similar to that of the salesman's particular firm?

Thirdly, *one should ask if there are any significant exceptions which have been overlooked.* Are there any firms of factors who are known to be offering consistent supplies of the product in question whom the customer has not taken into consideration?

This may seem rather elementary. But argument by induction is being used every day by buyers seeking reasons why they cannot place business. By recognising the type of argument whenever he meets it, the salesman can select the appropriate counter-arguments. If he can convince his client that he is genuinely mistaken in the objections he has raised, he is a lot nearer persuading him to place an order.

Here is another type of argument all salesmen are used to. The client says that the reason he will not place business with the salesman is that: 'I had a bad experience with a firm like yours some years ago.' This is called *argument by analogy*. The customer is asserting that there are similarities between the salesman's firm and the company with whom he had a bad experience. He is inferring that, because of this apparent similarity, both firms will behave alike in the matter of the quality of the product they supply.

The salesman should counter this by asking: (1) *are the similarities of the two cases cited necessary for the particular case advanced?* In other words, because the two firms are similar in *some* respects does this really prove that they must necessarily behave similarly in *all* respects? (2) *can it be said that the facts upon which the analogy is based are true?* This is just another way of asking the customer how sure he is that the other firm really is like the one the salesman represents.

It is astonishing how often one hears people making emphatic assertions the accuracy of which they could never hope to prove. When a buyer makes an assertion he cannot corroborate to justify an objection either to a product or a supplier he leaves himself open to counter-attack. If a client tells you that the price you have quoted is admittedly keener than that of your competitors but this makes him suspicious of the quality of your merchandise, he may be said to be arguing *from effect to cause*. 'It cannot be such a good product as your competitors are supplying or you could not afford to offer it to me at such a low price. I bought a small quantity at a similarly low price from someone else last year and it was rubbish.'

The *effect*, apparent to your client, is the poor quality of the product received last year. The *cause* (or so he argues) was the low price at which it was sold to him. To refute an argument from effect to cause one first asks *whether the cause advanced is not just another effect of the same cause*. Maybe the low price he was charged was just another effect of the real cause of the customer getting poor quality—namely, that the previous supplier did not know the market and had insufficient knowledge of both quality and value. Alternatively, one could ask *if the cause cited is associated with the effect merely by chance?* Which, in this instance, would be another way of suggesting that it was coinciden-tal that he got so-called 'rubbish' when he paid a lower price because imperfect goods are, on occasion, also sold at the standard market price. Thirdly, it should be questioned *whether the cause is something which existed before the effect*. In other words, could the customer necessarily deny that reliable merchandise had been sold to him both before and after this particular incident at a price lower than the normal market level?

Finally, a client will often seek *to argue from cause to effect* in support of an objection. 'I will not buy from you because you are a factor and therefore will not be able to provide me with the same technical service as a manufacturer.' The method of refuting an argument of this nature is, first, to challenge *the validity of the association between the specific cause and the specific effect*. Secondly, to query whether *some other cause may prevent the operation of the cause advanced*. Has the client considered that, although your firm is indeed factoring and not pro-ducing the product in question, you are manufacturing kindred pro-ducts and have a reliable technical service department comparable to that of your competitors?

Unaccustomed as I am . . .

To be able to speak fluently in public is a prized asset. A salesman who can get on his feet and with confidence address groups of people enhances his selling potential. Additionally, he may find he has the means to widen the horizons of his professional and social life. Good speakers are always at a premium and the man or woman with the facility to speak well in public is always in demand at meetings of trade associations, business conferences and seminars, plus a host of semi-social gatherings.

Those who have had little or no experience of public speaking often are gripped by nervous tension when they get up to address a group of people. Highly conscious of the fact that they are exhibiting themselves to the silent criticism of their audience they sense an almost paralysing fear that betrays itself in both speech and manner. One can, however, find reassurance in the following:

(*a*) This reaction is natural and common to most people;
(*b*) Silence on the part of your audience seldom indicates hostility— it is more often a sign of interest and attention;
(*c*) Tension in the speaker transmits itself to the audience. The more relaxed the speaker appears to be the more relaxed will the audience become which, in its turn, will help the speaker to *become* relaxed.

It is essential to know what you want to say. You should know your subject, by which I mean that you should think out what you want to say beforehand. Your address should have a theme. This will give it continuity and help you to gain and retain the audience's attention.

It is better usually to speak extempore with one's main items written on sheets of paper or on postcards numbered in sequence. It can be hazardous for the inexperienced speaker to read a speech. It takes considerable skill to put over a written speech. But it is equally a mistake to try to speak in public without adequate notes. So long as you have your sheets of paper or your cards, itemizing the main points you want to make, you can stop worrying about the possibility of 'drying up'. By speaking extempore, you can express yourself in your own words, modifying your phraseology in accordance with the mood of your audience. You will be able to sense the way the audience is receiving the speech. You can decide, if you think it appropriate, to expand your remarks on one item and reduce or even omit altogether, your references to another. Once you are actually before your audience you may well discover that a colloquial turn of phrase more adequately gets the point across than may have been apparent when preparing the speech. When one is working from a pre-prepared script it is often difficult to depart from it temporarily and find one's way back to it again without awkward fumbling.

Many inexperienced speakers have a tendency to gabble. Do not be in too much of a hurry. Try to develop a rhythm which will enable you to pause between items to glance at your notes. Speak out to the audience as much as possible with your eyes on them—not on your notes. Be friendly towards your audience! Put them at their ease. If the speaker shows embarrassment, individual members of the audience are likely to feel embarrassed *for him*. But once they are confident that *he* is confident, once they realize that they have nothing to fear, that he is not going to stumble or falter, they can relax and enjoy listening to what he has to say.

Most people comprehend, absorb and retain ideas and information better if they receive messages visually as well as orally. This is why many speakers delivering lectures on complex subjects frequently use what are called 'flip charts', consisting of several large sheets of paper clipped together on a backing board, on which they can write with crayon or felt-tipped pen. The speaker can use his chart or blackboard to emphasize a particular point. Sometimes, a single word written boldly on the chart will enable him to instil a dominant idea into the minds of his audience.

One should remember that public speaking is a performance. There are techniques for grasping and holding the audience's attention. The speaker's voice is vitally important. Vary the pitch and pace of your speech. Remember that you must give the audience time in which to take in what it is you are saying. You have been over and over the piece before and *you* know what it is all about. But the audience is hearing your words for the first time. Pause after you have made a significant point. A pause acts as a mental underlining that enables the point to register in the minds of your listeners.

Aim to interest and entertain the audience. This does not mean cracking jokes. It takes experience and skill to put a joke over successfully. But a touch of humour helps to personalize you to the audience. Very often, one is addressing strangers. They do not know you and, because most people are naturally polite, they will listen to you in silence unless and until you say something that tells them you have a sense of humour and that you want them to relax and laugh with you. People in a group usually have a suppressed desire to laugh even at the most trivial things. Let a cat walk across the stage during a performance of 'Hamlet' and the audience will giggle. Introduce a little humour into your speech on a normally serious subject and the little ripple of laughter it provokes will tell you that your audience is friendly and is with you.

Where possible, try to illustrate the points you are making with an appropriate anecdote or two. Just as the pictures in a newspaper help to enliven the printed page, so an anecdote enlivens a speech. It provides the audience with a moment's relaxation between the heavier items on which you want them to concentrate.

Public speaking, like driving a motor car, is a pretty awesome affair the first time you attempt it. But the more you do it the easier it becomes until the day arrives when you find yourself wondering why you ever thought it could be so difficult. Communication is what selling is all about and the capacity to convey ideas and information to groups of people should be part of every salesman's personal resources.

INDEX

Index